Praise for O Holy Night

Marian Rizzo breathes new life into this age-old Christmas carol. By weaving Bible culture and history with modern day examples, she gives the reader a deeper understanding of the meaning behind the lyrics. Each verse of the song becomes a powerful devotional message that inspires us to remember "the reason for the season." This is not a book you'll read once and lay aside; rather, it will become a traditional favorite that you'll reread each December to mark off the days until Christmas.
Doris Hoover, award-winning author of
Quiet Moments in The Villages, A Treasure Hunt Devotional

As you read Marian Rizzo's *O Holy Night*, and experience the depth of meaning in the words of the famous Christmas song, you will be drawn closer to Jesus and His love for you. So, brew a cup of tea, grab a comfy chair, and enjoy this inspirational treasure.
Delores Kight, award-winning writer and the co-author of
the children's picture book, Manny the Lamb.

What a great book for fans of the song *O Holy Night*. Marian Rizzo not only talks about the concepts found in each line of the song, but she makes it into a devotional by connecting the concepts with the scripture itself. In addition to that, she is a gifted story-teller. I was touched in a way I wouldn't have suspected by very brief stories about a flight attendant named Hope and the account of a cat and a dog playing with each other. And all of this is woven together into a beautiful Christmas gift. I recommend it.
Mario Villella, pastor of Good News Church Ocala
author of the booklet, Working Our Way Through Life;
What the Bible Says About Work.

O Holy Night

O Holy Night, *A Christmas Gift Book*, is based on the beloved carol, *O Holy Night*, originally penned as *Minuit, chrétiens* by poet Placide Cappeau and set to music by Adolphe Adam in 1847 as *Cantique de Noël*. The carol was translated into English in 1855 by John Sullivan Dwight.

Scripture quotations from The Authorized (King James) Version of the Bible. Public Domain in the United States. Rights in the Authorized Version in the United Kingdom are vested in the Crown. Reproduced by permission of the Crown's patentee, Cambridge University Press.

O Holy Night, *A Christmas Gift Book*
Copyright © 2020
Marian Rizzo

ISBN: 978-1-952474-18-7

Cover concept and design by Joanna Jones.
Used by permission. www.joannajonesart.simplesite.com

All rights reserved. No part of this book may be reproduced, stored in a retrieval system, or transmitted in any form or by any means—electronic, mechanical, photocopy, recording or otherwise—without the prior written permission of the publisher. The only exception is brief quotations for review purposes.

Published by WordCrafts Press
Cody, Wyoming 82414
www.wordcrafts.net

O HOLY NIGHT

A Christmas Gift Book

Marian Rizzo

WordCrafts Press

*This book was inspired by the sermons of Pastor
Mario Villella, of Good News Church Ocala,
and is dedicated to my dear friends,
Lois Liu Naftzger, who brightened my life with song,
and
Hope Tyson Lambert, a wonderful testimony of faith under fire.*

To God be the Glory!

*25 devotionals based on the lyrics
in the popular Christmas hymn*
O Holy Night

Begin reading on December 1 and finish on Christmas day

O HOLY NIGHT

O holy night, the stars are brightly shining,
It is the night of the dear Saviour's birth;
Long lay the world in sin and error pining,
'Till he appeared and the soul felt its worth.
A thrill of hope the weary world rejoices,
For yonder breaks a new and glorious morn;

Chorus

Fall on your knees, Oh hear the angel voices!
O night divine! O night when Christ was born.
O night, O holy night, O night divine.
Led by the light of Faith serenely beaming;
With glowing hearts by his cradle we stand:
So, led by light of a star sweetly gleaming,
Here come the wise men from Orient land,
The King of Kings lay thus in lowly manger,
In all our trials born to be our friend;

Chorus

He knows our need, To our weakness no stranger!
Behold your King! Before Him lowly bend!
Behold your King! your King! before him bend!
Truly He taught us to love one another;
His law is Love and His gospel is Peace;
Chains shall he break, for the slave is our brother,
And in his name all oppression shall cease,
Sweet hymns of joy in grateful Chorus raise we;
Let all within us praise his Holy name!

Chorus

Christ is the Lord, then ever! ever praise we!
His pow'r and glory, evermore proclaim!
His pow'r and glory, evermore proclaim!

✝

Introduction

We sing the lyrics. We love the music. But are we merely mouthing empty words and vain repetitions? Are we just humming the tune? Or do we honestly think about the underlying message? If we pay attention to what the lyrics are saying and concentrate on them in a worshipful attitude, the song takes on a whole new meaning.

Read the lyrics, line by line. Look closely at the words penned in 1843 by the French poet and wine commissioner, Placide Cappeau. As the story goes, he wrote the poem at the request of his priest for the church's Christmas mass. He focused the theme on the Second Chapter of the Gospel of Luke. With the help of a musician friend, Adolphe Charles Adams, the Christmas hymn, "Cantique de Noel," was born.

Later, John Sullivan Dwight, an avid abolitionist and magazine writer, brought it to America under the translated title, "O Holy Night."

These days at Christmas time, "O Holy Night" is performed in churches and concert halls throughout the world. Musicians accompany the singers on piano or organ. Some use worship teams, and some bring in full orchestras. Resounding praises fill the auditoriums.

In contrast is that moment of quiet when you stand alone in

your living room and look past the decorations and the lights, and even past the manger scene, and look ahead to the real reason for the season—the death and resurrection of Jesus, and salvation through His holy name.

†

O Holy Night

"*O* holy night." As you sing those words, perhaps a memory from your youth surfaces and you experience a brief moment of nostalgia. For many people, the song is reminiscent of the holiday season, its joyful celebrations, the brightly decorated homes and trees, nativity scenes, and candle-lit church services.

Throughout December, and often as early as November, "O Holy Night" is played in department stores, public parks, shopping malls, and, of course, in churches. People sing the words, or at least they hum the melody. Popular singers record it and sing it on television. Sometimes it serves as background music in holiday films.

For Christ followers, "O Holy Night" provides an added element for reflection. The holy night of the song goes beyond a moment in time. Sure, the words focus on a special child who was born in Bethlehem. But delve into the rest of the text and you'll see that it looks past the night of Jesus' birth to the day of His death. It turns from the manger to the cross, from the awestruck shepherds proclaiming the Messiah to an angry crowd crying "crucify him," from swaddling clothes to a bloodied robe, from an innocent babe to a sacrificial lamb, from humanity to deity. Yes, "O Holy Night" is much more than just another Christmas carol. It rings of forgiveness of sins and the hope of eternal life.

During one recent Christmas, my pastor, Mario Villella, of

Good News Church Ocala, spoke about how little the scriptures mention the birth of Christ. He pointed out that in the New Testament Jesus' birth is described in only two gospels—Matthew and Luke—while the rest of the New Testament speaks about His life, death, and resurrection.

Think about it. In Luke chapter 2, we read that Joseph took his family to Bethlehem to comply with the Roman census and pay taxes to Caesar. The chapter also speaks about Mary giving birth to her firstborn son in a stable, "because there was no room for them in the inn" (Luke 2:7b). A high point is the shepherds' miraculous encounter with angels who proclaim the birth of the Jews' awaited Messiah. After their mad dash to Bethlehem—with or without their sheep—and after seeing the holy child, the shepherds then went about spreading the good news. They may actually have been the first people to sing out the words, "O holy night."

Chapter 2 of Matthew's account talks about the visit of the wise men and King Herod's jealous vendetta against a child who would be king.

So we have two chapters that speak of Jesus' birth, and we have multiple New Testament passages that speak of His earthly ministry, and His death and resurrection, plus many Old Testament prophecies that point to the cross, the grave, and the resurrection of Jesus Christ.

During His ministry on earth, Jesus emphasized His purpose for coming here. He said He'd come "to seek and to save that which was lost" (Luke 19:10) and "to do the work of him that sent me" (John 4:34). That's why the night of His birth can be called a "holy night." It was the beginning of the fulfillment of God's great and wonderful promise to a fallen creation.

Moment of Reflection: What does the holy night of Christ's birth mean to you? Have you looked at the rest of the story? Meditate now on John 3:16, "For God so loved the world, that he gave his only begotten Son, that whosoever believeth in him should not perish, but have everlasting life." Consider God's purpose for sending Jesus to earth as a child to be born in a manger and destined for death on the cross. Then make a decision. Do you believe? Or are you simply following a ritual you learned as a child?

The reason we celebrate Jesus' birth is not because of what happened on that particular night but because of the rest of His life, and His death, and His burial, and His resurrection. The rest of the story is why we celebrate His birth.
   –Mario Villella, Good News Church Ocala

2

†

The Stars Are Brightly Shining

Have you ever noticed how bright the stars shine when you get away from the city with its tall buildings and neon lights? On some dark night get out in the country or another wide-open space and look up. Without a cloud in the sky the entire universe lights up like God's personal Christmas tree. Sometimes, especially in late summer, comets streak across the great expanse. Even the moon seems larger and brighter, at times reflecting a red or orange glow. And the stars map out a spectacular canopy of astrological formations.

I have known people who can point toward the sky and recite the names of some of those constellations. I personally have located the North Star, the Milky Way, and the Big Dipper. After that I'm lost amidst the breathtaking array of diamonds God has placed in the heavens.

Compare that umbrella of glittering sky with what the shepherds experienced on the night when Jesus was born. The lyrics of "O Holy Night" say the stars were brightly shining. The Bible doesn't mention the stars, but we do know it was nighttime, because Luke 2:8 says the shepherds were "keeping watch over their flock by night."

And, look at what happened next. "And, lo, the angel of the Lord came upon them, and the glory of the Lord shone round about them" (Luke 2:9).

So the black of night was suddenly interrupted by the shining glory of the Lord. God's glorious light must have been much shinier than a starlit sky, much brighter than a full moon, and much more astonishing than the streaking of comets. No wonder the shepherds were terrified. In addition to that startling bright light, an angel began to talk to them. But instead of frightening them further, the angel gave them a message of hope and joy.

Until that night, a different kind of darkness had prevailed on the earth. It wasn't a mere physical darkness. It was something else—spiritual darkness, which cannot be seen with the naked eye and does more than obscure the landscape. It threatens to destroy the human soul.

In scripture, darkness is equated with sin. For example, "Men loved darkness rather than light, because their deeds were evil" (John 3:19b). But look at the beginning of that verse. "And this is the condemnation, that light is come into the world" (John 3:19a).

Before Christ came to earth, a spiritual darkness prevailed. Then an angel brought good news. The Jews' long-awaited Messiah had been born. And He wasn't far away from the field where the shepherds were. The angel told them they would find Him lying in a manger in the town of Bethlehem, which was probably about a mile from where they were grazing their sheep. Shepherd's Field, a popular tourist site in Israel, could be the very location where the shepherds gathered on that glorious night more than two-thousand years ago.

The point is, they didn't have to travel far. They could actually go and see the Christ child that very night. These shepherds most likely had heard stories about the glory of the Lord. But it wasn't anything they'd ever seen before. Jesus entered a dark world and brought light. Like everyone else, the shepherds were living in spiritual darkness. They needed a savior. They needed to see the true light of God.

During His earthly ministry, Jesus declared Himself as "the light of the world" (John 8:12), Then He said, "He that follows Me shall not walk in the darkness but shall have the light of life."

The shepherds were among the first to see that light.

Sadly, much of the world still remains in darkness. But the holy night of Christ's birth sparked a shining moment in history. That initial blaze set off a whole generation of lights with one purpose, to spread the good news of salvation. Since then God has raised up a multitude of lights by igniting passion in the hearts of followers of Jesus Christ.

All over the world, on Christmas Eve, midnight services often include "O Holy Night" in the repertoire of music. The services usually end with a dimming of the lights. One person lights a candle and uses it to light someone else's candle, and so on, until the entire sanctuary is aglow.

That's what happens when people share the good news that Jesus came to earth as a human baby for the purpose of saving the lost. Because of His sacrifice, lives are changed. One candle can ignite many at a church service. Similarly, one changed life can affect many others, and they, in turn, can set a multitude on fire for God.

Moment of Reflection: If you are a believer in Jesus, your light of faith can brighten the darkness of a cold world. Have you hidden your light under a bushel? Have you allowed circumstances to diminish your flame? Rekindle your fire. Let your light of good works shine in the darkness and brighten the world around you and beyond.

See the lights, the stars over Bethlehem announcing the birth of the Prince of Peace. Lesser lights remind us that Jesus is the light of the world and that we are to let our light shine before men.
—Kirk Cameron, actor, filmmaker

3

✝
It is the Night of the Dear Saviour's Birth

Like everyone else, my life began with a birthday. Because my birthday happened in February, my mother always made me a heart-shaped cake with pink frosting. She did this every year for as long as I can remember. She even managed to whip up a heart-shaped birthday cake the year we got snowed in with drifts as high as our house.

When I turned seven years old, a reporter for our small-town newspaper came to my house and interviewed me about the birthday party I'd had that day. The next morning, a tiny two-inch brief touted my insignificant celebration like it was the social event of the year. I still have the clipping. It names several of my friends who attended. "Patty, Theresa, Donna, Joanne, and Jay-Jay." It went on to say, "We played button-button and pin the hat on the snowman." (Remember, it was the middle of winter in upstate New York.) Needless to say, I felt special.

Some of Jesus' followers did a similar thing with His birthday. They published it in the gospels of Matthew and Luke. Just like in my newspaper clipping, they mentioned people who were there—Mary and Joseph, of course, and a nameless innkeeper. Then there were the anonymous shepherds, plus the magi—also nameless and of an unknown number, though another popular

Christmas carol would have us believe there were three. Not only that, but those magi may have been as much as two years late for the party. Anyway, they brought presents—gold and myrrh and frankincense.

I have to concede, Jesus' birthday held far more significance than mine or any other human birthday. His birth gave us the promise of eternal life. Jesus didn't come to earth so people could eat cake, play games, and pop some balloons. He had a greater purpose. He said, "For the Son of man is come to save that which was lost" (Matthew 18:11).

We don't even know if He had multiple birthday parties, like we tend to do, year after year. He came here with a purpose that goes beyond people trying to remember your special day a year later. Or even ten years later. Or fifty. We remember Jesus' birthday because it promised us a second birth, and that's something to celebrate.

Jesus didn't necessarily expect to receive the gifts presented by the magi or any of the other accolades people bestowed on Him over the years. He came here to suffer and die so we might enjoy eternal life. Instead of receiving, He came here to give.

Notice what He said to the disciples in John 14:2, "In my Father's house are many mansions: if it were not so, I would have told you. I go to prepare a place for you."

Jesus came here, not to wear a party hat and open birthday presents. He came knowing His life would be cut short, that He would have only thirty-three birthdays and then he would suffer and die. He came not to receive but to give the best present He could offer—a place in heaven, which, ironically, requires us to experience another birthday.

Remember what Jesus told Nicodemus. He said, "Except a man be born again, he cannot see the kingdom of God" (John 3:3b). That means another birthday celebration has to take place. People need to experience a spiritual birth. No matter what they endured in the past, good or bad, no matter how much they regret former sins, they can start fresh by being born anew through Jesus Christ.

When that happens, a celebration takes place in heaven. The Bible says the angels rejoice over every sinner who repents (Luke 15:10). It's a different kind of birthday party, one you don't want to miss.

Moment of Reflection: Are you focusing on the day and the events that happened when Jesus was born, or are you looking ahead at the rest of His life and the rest of yours? For a moment, take your eyes off of the tinsel and the wrapping paper and all the other accoutrements of the holidays and focus on God's promise of eternal life. If you've accepted Jesus into your heart, you've already received the best gift of all. Salvation. It's a gift you can offer to others. Once you have it, you can't help but give it away.

Christmas isn't about getting, it's about giving, because God values generosity, not greed.

—Josh McDowell's Family Devotions
by Bob Hostetler and Josh McDowell.

4

✝

Long Lay the World in Sin and Error Pining

By the time Jesus made his entrance on earth, the world had gotten into a terrible state. Spiritual darkness prevailed. Idolatry had entered the land. The Roman Empire had expanded and had brought oppression on those who failed to obey the stringent rules. Sin was rampant. People strayed from the laws of God. They needed a deliverer.

The world's mess didn't happen overnight. It took place over centuries. In Noah's day, everything had gotten so bad, God finally threw up His mighty hands and decided to start over with eight people and a bunch of animals. Hundreds of years later, in the days of the judges, the cycle went from every man doing his own thing to crying out to the Lord in repentance and then back to every man doing his own thing again. And the cycle continued throughout the period of the kings. There were good kings and bad kings. Eventually the bad kings outnumbered the good kings. A few godly leaders, like Josiah, kept judgment at bay for a while. The prophets came along and people didn't listen to them. The separated nations of Israel and Judah eventually ended up in captivity.

During their years in captivity, the Jews fell under the control of several different powers—the Assyrians, the Babylonians, the

Persians, and the Greeks. Then, at the time of Jesus' birth, the Romans were in control.

The Jewish people were enslaved, not only by foreign powers, but also by the rules and regulations imposed upon them by their own religious leaders. They'd gone beyond the Law of Moses and were adding their own oral bylaws. The weight of all those rules had to feel oppressive. Where was the promised Messiah? Why hadn't He come to rescue them, as the prophets had predicted?

In answer to their pining, God sent His Son. But they didn't recognize Him. Jesus' birth meant nothing to most people of that day. The shepherds understood, but they'd had a miraculous revelation. The traveling magi had studied the stars and they believed. They came from afar. They even may have been Gentiles.

King Herod suspected something major had happened. He knew the Jewish people were waiting for the Messiah to come and rescue them. Like everyone else, Herod thought He would appear as a king. Surprise! He came as a baby, meek and innocent and totally dependent on his mother. When Herod heard reports about Jesus, he wanted to kill the child.

Contrary to what people believed back then, Jesus didn't come to deliver them from the oppression by the Romans or any other power that might invade their land. He came to overcome the sin and error that had left the people pining. Their own hearts threatened to bring more destruction on them than any outside power could.

Even today, we struggle with sin and error. Sadly, the world will not be completely free of problems until the end of times. We can blame Satan and his evil spirits. But, the truth is, we are probably our own worst enemy. We sin. We make mistakes. Even after we call ourselves "Christians," we fail. Just as Paul lamented in Romans Chapter 7, we are in a continuous battle against the flesh.

But Romans Chapter 8 quickly follows with promises from

the first verse all the way to the end of the chapter. It begins with, "There is therefore now no condemnation to them which are in Christ Jesus, who walk not after the flesh, but after the Spirit" (Romans 8:1). And look how the chapter ends. "For I am persuaded, that neither death, nor life, nor angels, nor principalities, nor powers, nor things present, nor things to come, Nor height, nor depth, nor any other creature, shall be able to separate us from the Love of God, which is in Christ Jesus our Lord" (Romans 8:38-39).

Moment of Reflection: When you lay your head on your pillow at night don't fall asleep without first reviewing your day and asking God to help you do better tomorrow. Stop pining over sin and error and reach for the only One who can rescue you. Ask him to help you repair a broken relationship, to make you aware of someone in need, and to love others the way God loves you. That's the way to freedom. Freedom from guilt. Freedom from selfishness. Freedom from senseless pining.

None but Jesus can give deliverance to captives. Real liberty comes from Him only...Let the Master say to me, "Captive, I have delivered you," and it is done forever.
    –Charles H. Spurgeon, Morning & Evening

5

✝
Till He Appeared
and the Soul Felt Its Worth

Can any of us say, "I have worth," and mean it? Can we look at our lives, past and present, and even our plans for the future, and declare any of our works worthy of praise? If we are honest with ourselves, we will admit that we fail, sometimes daily, sometimes horribly, sometimes so subtly nobody notices. The truth is, no matter how hard we try, we don't always have it all together.

Many times I have asked God, "Why?" But my plea is not over some tragedy I've experienced, although there have been plenty of those, like the time I was on life-support for three weeks. Even then, I don't recall ever asking God, "Why?"

When I do ask God, "Why?" it's most often because I have been blessed beyond my expectations, and I can't understand why God would be so kind to me, a sinner. If I take an honest look at my own condition, I would expect to receive God's judgment. Instead, He has blessed me over and over again, mercifully and with so much kindness I'm overwhelmed.

And so I say, "Why, God, are You being so kind to me? Why have You withheld the punishment I deserve and given me blessings I don't deserve?"

The truth is, it's not because I'm so great but because *He* is.

I'm not alone. Many of us, when we experience God's blessings, go through a similar scenario. We don't feel worthy to receive all the joy He's given us, first in salvation, and also in our daily lives. We go about our business and we hardly feel like we've earned any of the blessings we receive. Number them. First of all our children. Faithful spouses. Houses. Cars. Vacations. Even the family dog that makes you feel like the most important person in the world. They are all blessings from God.

Sure, you paid for many items with your hard-earned money. But who gave you that job? And what about things you can't claim to have earned? What about the apologetic phone call from an estranged friend who has come back into your life? What about the kiss you got from your wayward teen, the wild flower that popped up unexpectedly in your backyard, or the nest of baby cardinals in the tree out front? Such blessings had to come from the hand of a merciful and generous God who looks past our sins and flaws and sees our worth.

We might compare ourselves with others and come out ahead. Or we might fall short. We might look in a mirror, and, if we're honest, we might see a failure. But, what does God see? He sees a child who needs Him. It's kind of how we look at our own children. We look past their pathetic misbehavior and our hearts go out to them. We want to draw them to us, to nurture them and teach them and love them. That's how God feels about each one of us.

At Christmastime, there's a popular phrase that says, "Jesus is the reason for the season." People wear pins with those words printed on them. They send Christmas cards bearing the same message. Pastors sometimes quote that phrase while giving a sermon during the month of December.

It's true, Jesus is the reason for the season. He's the reason we put up manger scenes and decorations. He's the reason we give presents and sing Christmas carols. He's the reason we attend services, light candles, and worship Him in song and prayer.

But God had a different reason for the season. Our Heavenly Father looked down on us and saw our pathetic need. He saw our pain, our confusion, our insecurities, and our grief. He saw our sins and errors. He saw us pining, and His heart swelled with love for us.

So, what did He do? He sent His only Son to rescue us from our sins. And, He did it out of love. *We* were God's reason for the season. That's why Jesus came to earth to be born, to teach, to suffer and die, and to resurrect from the grave. He did it, not because we are worthy, but because God said we were worth the sacrifice.

Moment of Reflection: Have you been down on yourself for past mistakes? Have you been carrying guilt and regret far too long? It's time to realize your worth, at least as far as God is concerned. You are *His* reason for the season. You are the reason Jesus left His throne in heaven and came to earth to save you. He poured His own righteousness on the unrighteous. He gave His perfect life for the imperfect. He loved the unlovable, cared for the careless, and gave worth to the worthless. Accept His free gift and let Him know how grateful you are.

You are worth so much that God sent Jesus to die in your place on the cross.

—Charles Stanley, God's Way, Day By Day

6

†

A Thrill of Hope
the Weary World Rejoices

Are you weary of all the hype surrounding Christmas? Have you exhausted yourself running from one store to another to find the perfect gifts? Are your decorations in place? Did you climb ladders and stepstools? Did you untangle miles of peanut lights? Did you break your favorite ornament, burn the cookies, invite more guests than you have place settings for?

It's time to kick back and relax. And, it's time to get some perspective. Perhaps reach for that elusive thrill of hope. Think about the blessings you've received over the past year. Do some self-examination. Consider what you need to change—not to rearrange your living room furniture or buy a new car. What needs to be changed about *you*? If you're honest, you'll find a couple of things. But really, your life probably is pretty fine compared to what other people are going through at this time of year.

All of those items on your Christmas to-do list and all of those problems that surface during the holidays are minor distractions compared to what some people endure—not just at Christmas, but all year long.

I can't help but think about my friend, Hope, a beautiful Christian with a magnetic personality and a sweet spirit. Many years ago, we were both flight attendants. Sometimes we flew trips together.

Working with Hope was always an exhilarating experience. Hope was a tall, lovely African-American girl. She could have posed for the cover of a fashion magazine. Besides having a sweet, godly nature, Hope also had a strong persona that kept the most unruly passengers in line. I'll never forget the day we had a difficult male passenger and none of us other flight attendants could get him to cooperate. We called Hope to the rescue. In two seconds, she transformed that troublemaker into a meek little boy simply by removing her designer eyeglasses and staring down at him in that no-nonsense way of hers. She didn't have to say a word.

Years flew by faster than a 727, and here we are decades later, retired from our airline jobs, and on to other activities. I learned several years ago that Hope was diagnosed with multiple sclerosis. I immediately phoned her, expecting to hear a despondent voice on the other end of the line. Instead, her familiar sweet spirit came through, and I could picture the same beautiful, vibrant woman I used to fly with. Nothing had changed. Hope was still the spirited, godly woman I used to know.

At one point Hope admitted to me that she had always feared paralysis. But now that she'd been struck with a debilitating illness, she professed an unwavering trust in God. Her body had been weakened, but her spirit was still strong. She exuded a joyfulness that could only be attributed to her faith in God. The very place Hope dreaded has become her pulpit. It's within the confines of an unyielding body that she is able to proclaim an unwavering trust in her Savior.

I can't speak about Hope's wonderful testimony without also including a few words about her husband. Alex has demonstrated the deep and enduring love of a man who has stuck by his wife, in sickness and in health, caring for her even as her abilities began to decline. He is her rock in this terrible storm. He is a giant among men, a godly witness to the love of God filtering through one human being to another.

And so, isn't it appropriate that my friend was named Hope? She is "hope" personified. Even as her physical body continues to deteriorate, she has acquired that thrill of hope many of us seek but rarely find. I have learned so much from Hope. When my feet hurt or my head aches or when I'm bothered by some little problem, I only have to think of Hope. She has turned her bed into a pulpit and her illness into a powerful testimony.

Moment of Reflection: Is there someone in your life like Hope, who can't place an angel on top of a tree or make brownies or tie a bow on a gift? Thank God for their undying spirit and reach out to them. Visit them, telephone them, pray for them. Christ came to earth, not so we can throw parties around a ceramic nativity scene, or max out our credit cards, or eat way too much ham and sweet potatoes. He came to give us hope. In gratitude, we can extend that hope to friends and relatives who are hurting. That is why He appeared. That is why a weary world can rejoice.

Your story is the greatest legacy that you will leave to your friends. It's the longest-lasting legacy you will leave to your heirs.
     —Steve Saint, missionary to the Indians of Ecuador
               author of End of the Spear

7

✝
For Yonder Breaks a New and Glorious Morn

I love "O Holy Night." It's one of my favorite Christmas hymns. I also love the song, "Morning Has Broken," which can be played or sung at any time of the year. Both songs have catchy melodies and soul-stirring lyrics.

While "O Holy Night" makes a definite connection with the birth of Christ, "Morning Has Broken" speaks about a slightly different kind of awakening. The lyrics speak of birds, sweet rainfalls, sunlight, dew, Eden, and God's new day. They create an atmosphere of peace and tranquility. Surprisingly, those lyrics also fit in with the message "O Holy Night" conveys concerning the transition from weariness to rejoicing, from night to morning, from "sin and error, pining" to "a thrill of hope," and "a new and glorious morn."

Some people don't realize "Morning Has Broken," started out as a Christian hymn back in 1931, when it was composed by an English children's poet Eleanor Farjeon.

Forty years later, British entertainer Cat Stevens discovered it in an old hymnal. He changed the key, recorded it, and made it famous.

Something scriptural is going on with both of these songs. Genesis Chapter 1 and Psalm 8 tell of God's creation of the world, the birds of the air, the fish of the sea, sheep and oxen, and amphibians, and man. Like "Morning Has Broken," the song "O Holy Night" speaks of "a new and glorious morn" that broke on the morning after Jesus was born.

What could the next day have been like back then outside that stable? By this time, Mary was quietly pondering the experience in her heart (Luke 2:19). The shepherds had run off and were making known the birth of this special child (Luke 2:17-18). Did other curious folks flood into the streets of Bethlehem to catch sight of the Messiah? Was there a celebration? Did word spread throughout the countryside and beyond?

The scriptures don't say.

But one thing we can know for certain. No matter how dark the night, how heavy our burdens, how weary we may feel, on the horizon is a "new and glorious morn." Like it says in Psalm 30:5, "Weeping may endure for a night, but joy cometh in the morning." The child from heaven brought fresh hope, though few people realized it back then. But *we* know about it. We've heard the story for years. Churches in every city in America and in many other lands host Christmas services in celebration of the birth of Christ and the promises that came with that glorious event.

Jesus' birth was only the beginning. The next day brought a new and glorious morn. Even as we take down the strings of lights and pack away the nativity scene, the spirit of Christmas can live within us during the next week, the next month, the next year, and so on. It doesn't have to stop with one observance.

No matter what life is like at the present moment, no matter how dark the sky, how bleak the present, how uncertain the future, a new and glorious morn is on the horizon. Troubles will come. But God promised to wipe away all tears. He said there would be no more death, or sorrow, or crying, or pain. "For the former things are passed away" (Revelation 21:4).

Like the other song says, morning has broken. Birds sing, rain falls, dew awakens a garden, sunlight breaks through the clouds, and the people sing praises to God. Ultimately, Christ's birth brought about "a new and glorious morn" that will last forever.

Moment of Reflection: When things don't go exactly as you had planned, hang onto God's promises in the scriptures and trust Him for a better outcome. As the sun rises in the sky at the break of each day, Jesus brings new light to the world. As an exercise, take a slip of paper and write down anything that might be troubling you. Then slip the paper inside your Bible and give it to God. The One who made the heavens and the earth, the sky and everything under it—He can handle whatever you wrote on that little scrap of paper.

Want to hear about God? Step outside. The heavens are declaring, the sky is proclaiming the truth about the Creator. Nature shouts how awesome God is—from the tip-top of the sky to the deepest depths of the ocean.

—Linda Hang, Unfinished,
Devotions & Prayers for a Heart Under Construction

8

†

Fall on Your Knees

One of my favorite Bible verses is Micah 6:8, where the prophet says, "What doth the Lord require of thee, but to do justly, and to love mercy, and to walk humbly with thy God."

Those words are very convicting. Justice, mercy, and humility. Three things that are important to God and should be important to us too.

So, how do we "do justly?" By treating people the way we want to be treated. As Jesus said in Matthew 7:12, "Do unto others as you would have others do unto you" (paraphrased according to familiar usage).

What are some ways we can do unto others? Well, we can start by remembering.

Remember where you came from. As it says in the old hymn, "Remind Me, Dear Lord," sometimes you might have to allow Him to "roll back the curtain of memory," so you'll not forget where you came from and where you'd be if not for God's mercy.

You can treat others the same way you want God to treat you. Do justly to your spouse, to your children, to your friends and relatives, and even to your enemies. As it says in Romans 12:10, "Be kindly affectioned one to another with brotherly love; in honour preferring one another," and verse 18: "If it be possible, as much as lieth in you, live peaceably with all men."

Okay, that takes care of doing justly, but why should we "love mercy?" Because, as Jesus said in the Beatitudes, "Blessed are the merciful: for they shall obtain mercy" (Matthew 5:7). Hasn't He bestowed unimaginable mercy on every one of us? Don't mercy and justice go together? It seems you can't practice one without the other. If you want to be merciful, you have to do justly to that person. And you can't do justly without some measure of mercy.

It boils down to the second great commandment Jesus gave to the young lawyer in Matthew 22:39, "to love thy neighbor as thyself." That's not always an easy task. But Jesus didn't merely give us the commandment, He gave us His Holy Spirit to help us obey it. The scriptures are full of examples of people being merciful and just to others. Think about the Good Samaritan in Luke 10:30-42.

Of course, our best example of someone who bestows mercy is Jesus. As He was dying on the cross, He asked the Father to forgive those who were crucifying Him. At the same time, He was forgiving all of us.

Micah also says we must walk humbly with our God. True humility happens the moment we realize how very small we are in His presence. We are weak. God is powerful. We are sinners. He is sinless. We have flaws. He is perfect. We are mere mortals. He is the eternal God. Even a little baby in a manger was greater than we could ever hope to be.

Now comes the "fall on your knees" part of the song. Throughout scripture great and powerful men fell on their knees before God. The psalmist bids us to "worship and bow down" and to "kneel before the Lord our Maker" (Psalm 95:6).

Again, we can look to Jesus as our greatest example. Philippians 2:8 tells us, "And being found in fashion as a man, he humbled himself, and became obedient unto death, even the death of the cross." Jesus walked humbly on the earth from the day He was born and all the way to the cross.

Fall on our knees? You bet. Just like John did when he encountered Christ and then wrote about the experience in the book of Revelation. In fact, he didn't just fall on his knees, the Bible says he "fell at his feet as dead" (Revelation 1:17). That sounds like he was flat on the floor.

Some of us are too old or too lame to fall on our knees, much less sprawl flat on the floor. But even when we're not physically able to fall on our knees, we can symbolically do so. We don't have to put on a public display. The Bible tells us God sees the heart (1 Samuel 16:7). He knows when we're walking humbly before Him, though it may not seem obvious to anyone else. He knows when we are falling on our knees within our spirit, and that's enough. He cares more about the attitude than the action.

Moment of Reflection: Some people fall on their knees in the privacy of their bedrooms. Some do so as part of a congregational ritual. In either case, it's not the attitude of your physical body that counts. What's important is the attitude of your heart. Whether or not you fall on your knees is insignificant. The next time you say a prayer or sing a hymn or read a passage of scripture, bow before Him within your spirit. That's what matters to the King.

The response to the true unveiling of the glory and the majesty of God is always submission ... for to know Him is to immediately fall down in wonder, love, praise, and submission.
        –Joseph S. Carroll, *How To Worship Jesus Christ*

9

†

OH HEAR THE ANGEL VOICES!

My dear friend Lois can sing like an angel. I can attest to that from first-hand knowledge. It happened many years ago, when a terrible virus landed me in the hospital. We were in the boot camp stage of training with New Tribes Mission (now Ethnos 360). I ended up on life-support for twenty-five days, in ICU for five weeks, and in the hospital for two months.

I don't know if it was a corona-type virus but it sure acted like the one that struck the world in 2020. Besides giving me double pneumonia, the disease attacked nearly every organ in my body. I was dying.

In a last desperate attempt, the doctors decided to try therapeutic hypothermia. They induced a coma for forty-eight hours and lowered my body temperature. It was as if I had fallen into Lake Michigan. All my body functions stopped. When they revived me, the virus was gone and I was on my way to a slow recovery. They told me later that a virus won't live in extreme cold. The therapy killed the virus and I lived.

The doctors did a fine job, but I knew the real reason I survived. Friends and relatives were praying for me. Members of my church were praying for me. People around the world were praying for me. In fact, some of the jungle missionaries wrote that natives who had converted to Christ were on their knees in prayer for me. How awesome is that?

Also awesome was the arrival of my friend Lois who flew from California to Pennsylvania to see me for what she thought would be the last time. Her beautiful soprano voice was the first voice I heard when I awakened from the coma. She was singing the Michael Card hymn, "The Lord Bless You and Keep You," which is based on Numbers 6:24-26. "The Lord bless thee, and keep thee: The Lord make his face shine upon thee, and be gracious unto thee: The Lord lift up his countenance upon thee, and give thee peace."

In a way, I heard an angel's voice. Not the same voices the shepherds heard that night long ago, but the angelic sounding voice of my dear friend Lois.

As I opened my eyes, there she was, smiling down at me. Even though she was four months pregnant with her first child, she made the cross-country trip from California to Pennsylvania. That is a true friend. She could have stayed home and taken care of her unborn baby. She could have simply said she would pray for me. She could have sent her regards, and that would have been enough. But she did what a true friend does. She left the comforts of home and came to my side. And then she sang to me.

Only my immediate family could enter my room in ICU. I am of Italian/American descent. Lois is from Taiwan. She told the nurses she was my sister and guess what?! They let her in.

In truth, we *are* sisters. *Sisters in Christ.* She was the angel who welcomed me back to consciousness with a voice that could stir the heavens.

I imagine the angels' voices were similarly pleasing to the shepherds' ears. They, too, were awakened from darkness to light. In their case, the angels were announcing the birth of the Messiah, and no greater song has ever been sung.

In my case, Lois was singing God's message of encouragement and blessing.

Just as I will never forget Lois's kindness and the voice that awakened me from the coma, so also we should remember the angels' proclamation that brought a promise of freedom from another type of deathlike sleep—the sleep of ignorance and sin.

Read the passage in Luke 2:9-14 and notice the details: "The glory of the Lord shone round about them" (verse. 9); the angel said, "Fear not: for, behold, I bring you good tidings of great joy" (verse 10); and "For unto you is born this day in the city of David a Saviour, which is Christ the Lord" (verse 11); then the heavenly host praised God and said, "Glory to God in the highest, and on earth peace, good will toward men" (verse 14).

Moment of Reflection: Have you heard the angels' voices—not audibly, but in your heart? Just like my friend Lois came to see me when I needed her most, you can do the same thing for a friend. Maybe you won't sing to them—and maybe it's best if you don't. But you can be God's messenger of kindness, an angel so to speak. You can give them comfort during sickness, hope following loss, and love when they need it most. Sometimes it only means sitting quietly nearby. The main thing is, take a little time out of your holiday activities and just be there.

Believers, look up—take courage. The angels are nearer than you think.

–Billy Graham

10

✝

O NIGHT DIVINE! O NIGHT WHEN CHRIST WAS BORN
O Night, O Holy Night, O Night Divine

Let's take a trip back in time a little more than two-thousand years ago. Chapter 2 in the Gospel of Luke brings the setting to life. There was a field. Shepherds were there keeping watch over their flocks. The sheep probably were grazing. Or maybe they'd been rounded into a cove surrounded by rocks with only one way in or out.

The gospel also says it was nighttime. The song calls it a "holy night, a divine night." It might have been a dark, starless, moonless night. How else would the glory of the Lord shining about them have created such a stir? His light must have been really bright compared to the darkness all around them.

Angels appeared. They gave enough details for the shepherds to know exactly where to go and what to look for. The city of David? Apparently, everybody knew that meant Bethlehem. A babe wrapped in swaddling clothes? Nothing unusual about that. But, in a manger? That was the key. Who on earth would place a child in a manger?

What did those shepherds do? According to Luke 2:15-16, they said, "'Let us now go even unto Bethlehem, and see this thing which is come to pass, which the Lord has made known unto us.'

And they came with haste, and found Mary, and Joseph, and the babe lying in a manger."

The shepherds went, the Bible says, "with haste." I can't help but wonder, who looked after the sheep while they were gone? They couldn't take the entire flock with them. Maybe one or two shepherds stayed behind. Would you want to? After getting a message like that from angels, wouldn't you want to go with haste and witness this miraculous event?

It's easy for people to recreate the scene. Every December we pull the nativity set from the box in the attic. We go to a play and watch actors perform their parts—Mary and Joseph and the baby Jesus in the center. There might even be a live donkey or a cow inside the stable with them, although such a menagerie may not have existed at all. It makes more sense if the stable had been swept clean and the animals were grazing out in the field somewhere, like the sheep were doing.

After all, who would bed down in a cold stable with a bunch of filthy animals? Who would accept such a horrible setting for a birthplace?

Only one person I can think of. Only Jesus would have humbled Himself to such a degree. After all, didn't He also mingle with the lowliest people on earth? Didn't He touch lepers and bleeding women, the sick and even the dead? Didn't He allow Himself to be beaten and maligned and hung from a Roman cross for all to see?

But, this was supposed to be a holy night, a night divine. Why wasn't the Savior of the world, the King of the universe, greeted by kings and queens? Why didn't they open the doors of the palace and invite him in, create a soft bed for him with clean blankets, and offer food and lodging to his earthly parents? Why on earth did he spend the night divine in a filthy stable surrounded by shepherds who labored in one of the lowliest professions of that day?

Very likely they were clothed in shabby tunics with sheep dung clinging to the soles of their sandals. Despite their low estate, the shepherds had been given the honor of experiencing a rare visitation by angels who announced the birth of their Messiah, and an even more honorable opportunity to be able to go and see Him.

Yes, for the shepherds, it was a night divine, a holy night. And for Jesus, it was the setting for His entry into the world. But none of the humble circumstances were able to detract from the divine glory that took place on that holy night.

Moment of Reflection: This Christmas step aside from the ornaments and the colored lights and the table decorations and take a quiet moment to read Luke Chapter 2. Think about the One who left His throne in heaven to lie in a manger on His first night on earth. Imagine that you've traveled back more than two centuries, that you're standing face-to-face with the Savior of the world, the Lord of Lords, and the King of Kings. Now, isn't that divine?

I truly believe that if we keep telling the Christmas story, singing the Christmas songs, and living the Christmas spirit, we can bring joy and happiness and peace to this world.
  —*Norman Vincent Peale*

11

†

LED BY THE LIGHT OF FAITH SERENELY BEAMING

*I*n addition to the Holy Family, plus shepherds and any assortment of animals, most nativity scenes also include a trio of kings, along with their camels and expensive gifts. Though possibly not entirely accurate, the ceramic figures help to show the variety of souls the advent of Christ had touched. From the lowest to the highest in their society—shepherds to wise men—the first Christmas involved two of the most extreme classes of humanity of that day.

When people create their manger scenes, they usually group the wise men and their camels along with the shepherds and their sheep, and that's okay, because if we consider the Christmas story as a whole, the little details don't matter.

As the song says, "Led by the light of Faith serenely beaming," those magi followed a star by faith. They had no road maps, no Atlas, no GPS. Only faith and a star to lead them where they needed to go.

Take those words out of the first century and place them in modern times and they are no less true. No matter what our position in society, no matter how much or how little wealth we have, everyone is led to Jesus by the light of faith. Such faith doesn't announce an arrival with pomp and a marching band. It's "serenely beaming," which sounds like a rather subtle experience. By faith the shepherds and wise men went to Bethlehem to worship the arrival of the Savior, and here we are, more than two-thousand years later, and we can worship Him too, by faith.

The shepherds traveled a short distance, maybe a mile or two, to see the miracle of miracles. The wise men came a great distance to see Him. The shepherds came because angels appeared to them that very night. The wise men apparently knew the prophecy, and, after studying the stars, they followed the one bright star that would lead them.

People are led to Him today through other means. They read a passage of the Bible and a light bulb goes on in their heads. They sit in a church and listen to a preacher tell about this wonderful gift from God. They visit with a friend who knows the truth and imparts it. And so on. These are the angels and the guiding lights of today, and they are no less effective.

But, we know something the shepherds and the wise men didn't know back then. They had no idea this child of joy would die on a cross one day. We know it, because we know the whole story.

In that day and time, the Jews were expecting a champion, someone who would defeat the Romans and any other enemy that might oppress them. The shepherds had to wonder about the change in this eternal plan. Yet, they didn't question it. The Bible says they went with haste.

The magi were probably Gentiles. They traveled a great distance from other lands. They followed a bright light in the sky. Their hearts must have burst with joy when they arrived at their destination. Their long journey had finally come to an end. They had reached the place of the promise.

This baby was someone special. The wise men brought Him precious gifts. They bowed before Jesus knowing He was King of the Jews. And, when King Herod requested they come back with information about the child, they heeded a warning that came to them in a dream and they did not return to the palace. Their journey was over. They could return home and share the amazing story of their visit to Bethlehem.

Moment of Reflection: The wise men were led to Jesus by a star in the sky. People today are led by the "light of faith." The wise men placed their worldly gifts before the Christ child. How much more should we offer our gifts, our talents, our worship, and, most of all, ourselves? There are many ways to give gifts to the Lord. We can help others, especially at this time of year when so many are unable to join the holiday celebrations. Find one person to help. One family. One lonely individual. The blessing you receive will shine like the magi's star.

I will love the light for it shows me the way, yet I will endure the darkness for it shows me the stars.
                                                             –Og Mandino

12

†

With Glowing Hearts by His Cradle We Stand

When my children were babies I spent an unreal amount of time standing by their cradles, watching them sleep, checking to make sure they were still breathing. My heart glowed with love for them.

Then, whenever I took them out with me—to the park, to the mall, or pushing the stroller around the neighborhood—I sometimes turned their seat around so I could keep an eye on them. I was afraid someone would try to steal them or that something would happen to them when I wasn't looking. I was one paranoid mama.

Even as they grew older, I continued to hover over my embarrassed teenage daughters. I was a true-life "helicopter mom," especially with Joanna, because she was an independent child, off and running pretty much from the day she was born!

Our second daughter, Rachel, died when she was three weeks old. She was three months premature and succumbed to a bad infection. Though I still grieve over the loss, there came a day when I asked God to send me a baby I could hug. Joanna was already doing her own thing, and I'm proud of all she has accomplished. But I needed a hugger.

That was when God sent us Vicki. She has Down syndrome and she is the world's greatest hugger. She's now thirty-five years old (going on twelve), and she still gives me hugs every day. God really does answer prayer, doesn't He? The Lord knows what we need, and His plan is always perfect. For me, it's an honor and a blessing to care for Vicki every day.

God also had a plan for the child He sent Mary and Joseph. They both knew Jesus was the expected Messiah, the Son of God. An angel had told Mary. Joseph had learned about it in a dream. Then God let other people in on that fantastic birth announcement.

The shepherds received a message from angels. When they left the field to go to Bethlehem, they knew they were on their way to see something truly miraculous. Then they entered the stable and approached the manger. Their hearts must have glowed at the sight of the newborn child of God.

The wise men, too, must have experienced an overwhelming sense of awe. What must it have been like to get that close to the Christ child? Did He open His eyes and gaze back at them? Did He smile? Did God's holy light descend upon Him, verifying who He was, like the spirit that settled on Jesus like a dove thirty years later at His baptism? (Mark 1:9-11) John the Baptist's heart must have really glowed at that moment.

Once, during His earthly ministry, Jesus singled out His apostles, Peter, James, and John, to witness something miraculous when He was transformed before their very eyes. Matthew 17:2 says that Jesus' "face did shine as the sun, and his raiment was white as the light." So overcome by what they had seen, the disciples fell down on their faces. The amazing vision must have left their hearts glowing for a long time after.

What a privilege they had been granted, to be able to walk beside the Lord and to be let in on so many secrets. Are you aware that God has revealed many of those secrets to you? You can read about them in His word, the Holy Scriptures.

All those amazing events the people in the Bible experienced can be yours too. You can join the apostles on the Mount of Transfiguration. You can kneel before the cross on Calvary, dine with Jesus on fresh-caught fish on the banks of Galilee, walk beside Him on the dusty road to Emmaus, and stand before His cradle with your heart glowing.

When we set up a manger scene, we shouldn't just arrange the pieces like little girls do when they put furniture into a doll house or like young boys do when they build something out of Legos. These wooden or ceramic or plastic parts of a nativity set are not playthings. They represent a fantastic work of God. Set Mary and Joseph in their usual places, one on each side of the manger. Arrange the shepherds and wise men, the cattle, the donkeys, the sheep, and all the other related items as you will. Perhaps an angel came with your set.

If you're like me, I have everything set up before Christmas and I add the babe on Christmas morning to complete the manger scene. But the truth is, a manger scene is just that—a scene. It's not an altar. It's not an idol. It's simply a reminder of what happened two-thousand years ago. That was only the beginning. The end is still ahead. Jesus has promised to return one day. Knowing that should set your heart aglow.

Moment of Reflection: When was the last time you paused by a nativity scene and thought about what the figures represent? Perhaps it's time to read again the story as told in Matthew Chapter 2. Allow your heart to glow with love and appreciation for what God did in sending His only begotten Son to earth so you might live with Him in eternity.

No time is more profitably spent than that which is set apart for quiet musing, for talking with God, for looking up to heaven.
—Mrs. Charles E. Cowman, Streams in the Desert

13

✝

So, Led by Light of a Star Sweetly Gleaming
Here Come the Wise Men from Orient Land

The wise men. The magi. One particular Christmas carol says there were "Three Kings." We don't really know if they were kings. They may have been a type of royalty in order to qualify for an audience with King Herod. Wise men could do that too. Most kings had their personal prophets and advisors. The Bible says they were wise men, and that's good enough for me.

The scriptures also say they came from the east. That same Christmas carol says, "the Orient." Sounds like they may have been Gentiles. They could have come from beyond the Jordan River from Peraea, a territory that belonged to Herod the Great, or they might have come from the ten cities of the Decapolis, or what we know today as Iraq and Iran, maybe even as far east as Afghanistan. Isn't it ironic that people from those lands may have had an opportunity to know the truth way back then, even without telephones, telegrams, and televisions? I have to wonder what the wise men did with that knowledge. Did they bring it home with them? The scriptures don't say what the wise men did after they left Judea.

Not only that, the Bible doesn't say how many wise men there were. People assume there were three because they brought three gifts: gold, frankincense, and myrrh. There could have been four or five wise men, or perhaps a dozen or more. Maybe even hundreds. Nobody knows.

Nor does the Bible say when the wise men made the trip. For years, we've included them in our nativity scenes. But, the truth is, it may have taken them up to two years to arrive in Bethlehem. The Bible says Jesus was in a "house" by this time. The Greek word, *oikion* is different from the word for manger, *phatne*, which could also be translated "stall" or the place where the manger was. By the time the wise men got there, Jesus could have been a curly-haired toddler.

But, does it really matter whether there were three visitors or more, or if they were kings or smart guys, or if they found the child in a house or a stable? Does it matter if Jesus was a newborn babe or two years old? What matters is that these men had traveled a great distance to come and worship Him, and they had brought precious gifts, some of which, like myrrh, also were used in the preparation of the dead for burial. Could this gesture have been a type of prediction of what was to come?

The wise men had followed a star. They must have known something about astronomy. Even today astronomers talk about some sort of conjunction of planets that may have occurred at that time. Again, nobody knows for sure what created this great light the wise men followed. Whether it was a real star, or planets, or a miraculous light placed in the sky by God, it's not as important as the end result. That light took the wise men directly to the place of Jesus' birth.

The wise men came to worship the Christ child. And, they were wise enough to heed a warning in a dream and not return to Herod, for it wasn't long after their visit that the evil king sent his men to Bethlehem to kill children "from two years old and under" (Matthew 2:16). Even Herod suspected there was something happening.

He must have known the prophecy. He feared that another king had come to overturn his reign.

Just as the wise men made time to worship the Christ child, you can do that too. You don't need to set up a manger scene. You don't need a star to lead you to Him. You don't need to bring Him gifts. What He wants more than anything is your heart. You can come to Him empty-handed. *He* is the gift-giver. *He* is the One who blesses. Open your hands and watch how He fills them. Better yet, open your heart. He'll fill that too.

Moment of Reflection: Pause now to meditate on what Christmas means to you. Consider how Jesus came to earth as a little baby so He could live as a human and ultimately die on the cross to pay for our sins. Like the shepherds and the wise men, you've been invited to receive Him. If you've accepted Him, you already are experiencing the peace and joy of salvation. If you are troubled, go beyond the manger and lay your burden at the cross. See Christmas for what God intended it to be—a path to salvation and wholeness.

The star was so beautiful, large, and clear, that all the other stars of the sky became a white mist in the atmosphere. And by this they knew that the coming was near of the Prince foretold in the prophecy.
–Henry Wadsworth Longfellow, The Three Kings

14

†

THE KING OF KINGS
LAY THUS IN LOWLY MANGER

I get lost nearly everywhere I go. I'm confused when someone tells me I need to head west, or if they say my destination is just around the next bend. If I'm supposed to turn right I inevitably turn left. I've even gotten lost in my own neighborhood. Once I drove around for four hours trying to find my way home from a friend's house. I have to admit, GPS has given me hope.

In the Bible you'll often read that people went "up to Jerusalem." Now Jerusalem was south of Galilee, so it seems the passages should say "down" to Jerusalem, doesn't it? Here in the U.S. we say someone is going "down" when they travel from New York to Georgia and "up" when they go from Florida to Maine. But in Israel, "up" doesn't mean north, it means into the mountains. Jerusalem is located on one of the highest mountains in that part of the world.

Consider how far Joseph and Mary had to travel to obey Caesar's census. Luke 2:4 says Joseph "went up from Galilee, out of the city of Nazareth, into Judea, unto the city of David, which is called Bethlehem; (because he was of the house and lineage of David)." They not only went "up" into the mountains, they traveled nearly eighty miles. Mary was nine months pregnant. Paintings show her riding on a donkey. Maybe she did. Maybe she didn't. Either way, walking or riding, it had to be one horrendous trip.

They could choose between two main routes. One traveled along a western road that went through Samaria and into the hill country. The other followed a longer route to the east along the Jordan River. Either way would have taken several days. Today you could drive the distance in a couple of hours.

Notice that they made the trip without road maps and GPS. They were accustomed to making that journey. All their lives they'd been required to go to Jerusalem regularly for certain festivals, such as the Passover. This time it was so Joseph could register for the census and pay a tax to Rome.

Little did they know that when they arrived at their destination they would have nowhere to stay. Already they'd been camping out on the trail for the last three or four days. It's not like when I go to see a friend, she welcomes me with a cup of coffee and a hot meal. Mary and Joseph didn't even get a comfortable room. And she was about to deliver their baby.

It's mind-boggling to think that the God of Heaven, the King of the Universe, the Lord of all, should humble Himself so profoundly as to settle for a dirty stable. What's more, He chose an obscure little town called Bethlehem to make His entrance into the world. Note the prophecy in Micah 5:2: "But thou, Bethlehem Ephratah, though thou be little among the thousands of Judah, yet out of thee shall he come forth unto me that is to be ruler in Israel; whose goings forth have been from of old, from everlasting."

Bethlehem Ephratah, former home of Ruth and Boaz, Obed, and Jesse, and the birthplace of David who would be king of Israel. The line of Christ continued through Solomon and his son Rehoboam and on through a series of kings. Though, in time, those kings made their residence in Jerusalem, Bethlehem had been chosen as the birthplace of the King of Kings and the Lord of Lords.

How did the angel refer to this place when speaking to the shepherds? "For unto you is born this day in the city of David a

Saviour, which is Christ the Lord" (Luke 2:11) The angel took it for granted that the shepherds would know the "city of David" was none other than Bethlehem. Nobody had to draw the shepherds a map.

God had deemed that His Only Begotten Son would start His life in a cold and dirty stable. The holy child spent His first night on earth in a manger where animals were probably fed only a few hours before. That was the beginning of the promise. Thirty-three years later Jesus would end His time on earth nailed to a cross. Yet He chose the manger. He chose the stable. And, in the end, He chose the cross. He did it for us.

Moment of Reflection: When you set up your nativity scene, think about what it took for Joseph and Mary to make that long journey. Compare their situation with yours. Next to that cold and filthy stable your castle seems pretty cozy, doesn't it? And your bed? Isn't it a little more comfortable than a feeding trough cut out of a block of stone? Now think about what Jesus left behind. He left his throne and the comforts of heaven, was born into poverty so He could provide the riches of heaven to those who would receive Him.

Just as Our Lord came into human history from outside, so He must come into me from outside. Have I allowed my personal human life to become a "Bethlehem" for the Son of God?
  —Oswald Chambers, *My Utmost for His Highest*

15

†

In All Our Trials
Born to be Our Friend

Some friends stay for a little while and leave a sweet memory behind. Some are soon forgotten. Then there are those special ones who are there for a lifetime and beyond.

Such was the case with my friend Cindy. We knew each other for 50 years and were best friends for 40 of those 50 years. Cindy was the kind of friend that was closer than a brother (or a sister in this case). Our friendship accurately portrayed the words of Romans 12:15: "Rejoice with them that do rejoice and weep with them that weep."

Cindy died in 2019 of a fast-moving form of ALS. But our friendship didn't die with her. I still remember with clarity our times together. Sometimes I find myself choked up with tears and sometimes I laugh out loud, like we used to do until tears were running down our faces and our ribs ached. I count myself very blessed to have known someone like Cindy.

An Irishman named Joseph Scriven wrote about an even greater friend in 1820. His hymn, "What a Friend We Have in Jesus," is sung in churches and campgrounds and Sunday school classes to this day.

As the story goes, Scriven wrote those words in the midst of terrible tragedies, including the death of his fiancée who drowned on the eve of their wedding. Here was a broken man who could have lost his faith in God, yet he turned instead to the only One who could provide the comfort he needed. He reached out to Jesus and called him "friend."

Scriven's lyrics tell us Jesus bears all our sins and griefs. Not just some of them, but all of them. That's right. We can carry all our burdens to Jesus. He will take our trials, our troubles, and our temptations. He is a faithful friend who will share our sorrows. He knows our every weakness and He will be our refuge and our shield. So many promises in only three stanzas.

Scriven was suffering emotionally when he wrote those words. How many of us, after experiencing a terrible tragedy, can call Jesus a friend? When we've lost a loved one, can we sing the lyrics of Scriven's hymn and mean them? Do we feel Jesus' comforting arms when we're bowed under an agonizing grief?

Think about your real-life friends, the people who run to you with warm hugs and gentle words when you've lost someone dear. They may not know what to say or do, but they are there. And you very likely do the same for them when tragedy strikes their home.

Many years ago, divorce left me with two daughters to raise. My oldest was a teenager. My youngest has special needs. Christmas was coming. I didn't feel like singing "O Holy Night," or "What a Friend We Have in Jesus," or any other song. I did thank God for providing me with a good job, but it wasn't enough to make a happy holiday for my kids.

An envelope miraculously appeared in my mailbox at work. It contained $100, an anonymous gift from my coworkers. A neighbor gave us a box of food provided by his church. Dear ones like Cindy sent presents and called to wish us well. The truth is, Jesus was being my "friend" through other people.

Though still grieving the death of my marriage, for the sake of my girls, I put up our artificial Christmas tree, decorated it with lights and homemade ornaments, and set out our nativity scene. It was a shining representation of another gift, one that came directly from God. It was His Son, Jesus Christ, my Savior.

My situation was far more comfortable than what Jesus experienced on His first night in Bethlehem. Think about it. I had a warm house and friends and relatives to encourage me. The King of Kings left His throne in heaven, took on the form of a human baby, and settled for a lowly stable on a hillside in Bethlehem. He felt the cold of night. He smelled the waste from dirty animals. He faced the wrath of Herod, the rejection of a godless world, and the suffering and anguish of crucifixion.

And He did it all so He could be called our Savior. Not only that, but he's the Prince of Peace, Holy God, King of Kings, and yes, as Scriven's song says, He's our friend.

Moment of Reflection: And so, we have in the manger a human baby, a holy God, a Savior, and also a friend. Try to relate to Him on each of those levels. Envision Him as God in the flesh, a human example of how to live a holy life. Think of Him as the Savior who suffered and died on the cross so we might live forever. And see Him as a friend, someone you can go to with problems, plans, and everyday needs. But never lose sight of who He truly is—Almighty God, King of Kings, and Lord of Lords.

He, at whose voice heaven trembles, even He, Great as He is, knows how to stoop to me.
–Madame Guyon, from a poem titled God's Glory and Goodness, in the book, Experiencing the Depths of Jesus Christ

16

†

HE KNOWS OUR NEED, TO OUR WEAKNESSES NO STRANGER!

Does Jesus really know our need and our weaknesses? Hebrews 4:15 says He does. The verse tells us He was "in all points tempted like as we are, yet without sin." Not only that, but, when He was in the form of man, "He humbled himself and became obedient unto death, even the death of the cross" (Philippians 2:8).

Christ understands our life situations far better than we might think. He probably caught colds. He must have been hungry. After all, he ate fish, and bread, and lamb. He thirsted. We know this for sure because of the statement He made on the cross in John 19:28. What's more, He probably endured stomach aches, mosquito bites, and sore feet from all the walking He did back and forth from Galilee to Jerusalem, a distance of nearly eighty miles!

He enjoyed time with His friends, He endured the taunts of His enemies, and He even feared the judgment that was about to come upon Him. He could have avoided the bad stuff. Nevertheless, he accepted the frailness of humanity on our behalf. He took on the likeness of man, reached out to man, and then died for man.

The difference between the human Jesus and the human us is that we succumb to temptation. As the Bible says, He was tempted but did not sin. Read about it in Matthew 4:1-11. The passage describes Jesus' face-to-face encounter with Satan, the tempter, and it took place after Jesus had endured forty days and forty nights with nothing to eat or drink. We humans struggle with temptation even when we're well-fed. We certainly wouldn't have the strength to fight back under the same circumstances Jesus endured.

When I'm suffering from an attack of hypoglycemia, I'll grab anything to eat, even foods that aren't good for me, like a candy bar or a bag of potato chips. Likewise, when I am down in the dumps, I'll be open to anything that will lift me up—pats on the back or words of praise—whatever. I'll take it all.

We crumble under trials. Jesus never did. He did not allow trials and temptations to diminish who He really was—the King of Kings, the Creator of the universe, God in the flesh.

As He prayed in deep anguish on the Mount of Olives minutes before his arrest, even though He could have summoned legions of angels to rescue Him, He submitted to the Father's will. That kind of strength and commitment is far beyond human ability.

Throughout His life and His approaching suffering and death, Jesus remained constant. He accepted the pain that comes with being human in a cold and ruthless world. And He accepted the end that had been mapped out for Him from the moment He was born, perhaps even from the moment of man's first sin in the garden of Eden.

While I should find joy in the fact that Jesus paid the price for my sins and opened the doors of heaven to me, it's actually a bitter-sweet kind of joy. On the one hand, I'm grateful for Jesus accepting my judgment and saving me from eternal death. But, on the other hand, I'm struck with the painful awareness that my sins helped to nail Him to the cross.

Maybe you've also found Christ's sacrifice brings a bitter-sweet kind of joy. The good news is, on top of eternal life (which should have been enough), Jesus also gave you the ability to deal with the trials and tribulations of the world you live in. You have access to

Christ's strength and His perseverance. When illness threatens to destroy your body, you don't have to let it destroy your spirit. When people accuse you unfairly, you don't have to retaliate in equal fashion. When temptation comes—and as certain as you remain in this earthly body, it will—you don't have to give in to it. You can bow before the Lord, call on His strength, and claim victory.

Moment of Reflection: Are you experiencing a trial? Is temptation knocking at your door? Whatever your situation, through faith you can call upon the name of the Lord for strength, for perseverance, and for wisdom to deal with whatever is oppressing you. Like Scriven's song says, He is no stranger to our needs and our weaknesses. Arm yourself for the battle. Memorize selected verses of scripture, like Isaiah 26:3, "Thou wilt keep him in perfect peace, whose mind is stayed on Thee: because he trusteth in Thee." You'll be glad you did.

Christ was not only God, but he was God and man in one person.
–George Whitefield

17

†

BEHOLD YOUR KING!
BEFORE HIM LOWLY BEND!
Behold Your King! Your King! Before Him Bend!

In the previous chapter, we looked at Jesus' humanity. Now, look at Him again, but this time, see Him as King. He sits on a throne. He wears a crown. He is worshiped by multitudes. He rules the universe and everything in it.

But at one time, a little over two-thousand years ago, He chose to leave His throne and the comforts of heaven to be born in human flesh and to endure a life of rejection and then face a horrible death. It's hard to comprehend that anyone would agree to such a drastic commitment. I doubt that I would. I hate pain. And, like many, I would probably fight to live.

But Jesus didn't fight. He accepted the suffering we deserve. When the time came for Him to be arrested and face a demeaning trial, He didn't fight back. Though He could have saved His own life, He refrained from doing that.

His love for us and His obedience to the Father gave Him the strength to follow through with His Father's plan. The entire scenario is mind-boggling. Here was a king who, in place of a crown of gold, he accepted a crown of thorns, and in place of a scepter, he accepted a cross.

It's reminiscent of Charles Wesley's famous hymn, "And Can

It Be That I Should Gain." The lyrics he wrote in 1738 we still sing today. Most of the time, tears come to my eyes and I get so choked up I can hardly finish the refrain. The truth overwhelms me.

Consider the words that poured from Charles Wesley's heart through his pen onto a piece of parchment, words that still reverberate in churches and chapels throughout the world.

> *"And can it be that I should gain*
> *an interest in the Savior's blood?*
> *Died He for me, who caused His pain—*
> *For me, who Him to death pursued?*
> *Amazing love, how can it be,*
> *That Thou, my God, shouldst die for me?*
> *Amazing love, how can it be,*
> *That Thou, my God, shouldst die for me?"*

Even now, as I write these words, a profound realization sweeps over me. To think that the King of the universe would die in my place. The sinless God gave His life for the sinner. The blessed Savior took the place of the lost. The holy King suffered for the spiritual pauper.

Later in the same hymn, it says, "He left His Father's throne above, So free, so infinite His grace—Emptied Himself of all but love, And bled for Adam's helpless race."

Do those words mean anything to you? What about the way the hymn ends with these words: "Bold I approach th' eternal throne, and claim the crown, through Christ my own."

There you have it. A crown awaits us, maybe even many crowns depending on our service and our loyalty to the King. The Bible lists five crowns: "The Incorruptible Crown" (1 Corinthians 9:25); "The Crown of Rejoicing" (1 Thessalonians 2:19); "The Crown of

Life" (Revelation 2:10); "The Crown of Righteousness" (2 Timothy 4:8); and "The Crown of Glory" (1 Peter 5:4).

And, what will we do with our crowns? The Bible says the twenty-four elders will cast their crowns before the throne (Revelation 4:10), so I imagine we'll probably do the same thing. The King is going to give us crowns and we're going to give them right back to Him. How wonderful is that? And, how appropriate, for we would have nothing at all if not for Him.

A few years ago, I commissioned my daughter Joanna, a talented artist, to paint a picture of Jesus wearing a gold crown and I asked her to work beneath the gold a bloody crown of thorns. She did a fabulous job. The painting now hangs in my hallway across from my home office, a ready reminder of the King of Kings who gave His life for me.

That painting stands in contrast to the nativity scene around the corner in my living room. One shows a baby lying in peaceful slumber. The other shows a King who suffered and died on the cross. From the manger to the cross. From Christmas to Easter. From Christ child to Savior. But always King of Kings and Lord of Lords.

Moment of Reflection: When you look at a nativity scene, what do you see? A decorative arrangement with ancient looking figurines? A young couple with a little baby? A grouping of shepherds and wise men? Look closer. Focus on the child in the manger. Picture Him with a crown of gold on his head. Then look beyond the gold crown and see the thorns. He endured so much to connect with us, to guide us, and to teach us, and ultimately to prepare us for eternity. Thank Him today for His indescribable gift.

The Lord Jesus Christ Himself is our perfect example, and He knew no divided life. In the Presence of His Father He lived on earth without strain from babyhood to His death on the cross.
—A.W. Tozer, The Pursuit of God

18

†

Truly He Taught Us to Love One Another

For years I had a dog and a cat at the same time. We all lived in one house together. And we all got along just fine. Even the dog and the cat.

I've heard it said that dogs and cats are total opposites. They're not supposed to get along. Dogs are loyal. They thrive on attention. They want to play with you, chase the ball, beg for treats, jump on your lap. Dogs need constant reassurance. They wait by the front door until you return home from wherever you went. Then they follow you around "like a little puppy dog," as the saying goes.

Cats are more independent. They can disappear for days at a time and then come home perfectly content to curl up on your favorite easy chair or on the foot of your bed. Most of the time they go about their own business. They hardly ever come when you call, unless you're opening a can of food. Then they weave in and out between your ankles, nearly tripping you until you set their dish on the floor. At that point they don't know you anymore.

Dogs eat constantly. Cats nibble. Dogs will lick the bowl clean. Cats leave part of their meal for later. You have to keep the cat's bowl away from the dog or the food will quickly disappear. I've been told that cat food is not good for a dog and vice versa.

I've always preferred dogs, but, not to be unfair to cats, I did have several loveable kitties over the years. Two of them in particular liked to cuddle almost like dogs do. Fonzie was a little stray runt we adopted from a feral litter. Tripod also was a rescue after a car hit him and smashed his leg and part of his jaw. Both cats seemed to appreciate their new home. They were lovable.

Beanie, our yellow Lab/mix, and Tripod, our three-legged cat, got along as well as a dog and cat can. Beanie looked like Old Yeller, the dog from the movie. He was big and bulky. Tripod was a frail little, spikey-haired kitten.

The two of them rolled around on the floor and played like the best of buddies. Beanie played only with his head and one paw. It was as if he knew that if he used his whole body he'd probably crush Tripod. He seemed to understand their different sizes and abilities. Meanwhile, Tripod played with his whole body. He'd lunge at Beanie with his three legs extended and would even thrust his head inside Beanie's mouth. Somehow, they never hurt each other. After all, it was playtime.

Later, we'd find Beanie asleep with his body curled into a half circle and Tripod snuggling up inside. It wasn't long after Beanie died that Tripod's health began to deteriorate. He became really quiet, like he missed his cuddly playmate. Tripod died about six months after we lost Beanie. We buried them next to each other in the backyard.

People are kind of like dogs and cats. Sometimes we meet people who rub us the wrong way. They may say something rude. Maybe you sense a negative spirit. Jesus said we are to love one another. He said to pray for our enemies. Maybe we don't live in the same house (and maybe we do). Maybe we play on the same team, or work in the same office, or take the same classes in school. Perhaps we attend the same functions, or shop in the same market, or ride on the same bus, or sit next to each other in church. Somehow, we're thrown together with the wrong people.

Whatever the case, we're always going to encounter folks we don't care for as much as we care about others. If we want to obey the scriptures, we'll find a way to love them the same way Jesus loves us. It may begin with a simple prayer. Or a kind word. Or even going out of our way to help the person. We can do all of those things under the power of God's Holy Spirit.

We can mend that imaginary fence that rose up between us and that nasty neighbor. We can eliminate the unseen wall between our station and that of the coworker. We can pull down the barriers, smooth over the offenses, and, as Doctor Phil often says on his TV show, "Be the hero." Every situation, every conflict is looking for someone to step up and be the hero.

Sometimes, it's up to us to make the first move. But we don't have to do it alone. We can call on the Savior who tore down the walls of opposition the day He went to the cross.

Moment of Reflection: Take a moment now to think of someone who has offended you. Put aside your ill feelings, and say a prayer for that person. You may not mean it at first, but just as Jesus blessed His enemies while He hung on the cross, you, too, can ask forgiveness for those who have harmed you. You can repair divisions and offer godly love to the offender. Otherwise, how can we rightfully say, "Forgive us our debts, as we forgive our debtors," as Jesus taught in Matthew 6:12? If we truly want to follow Him, we should do as He did.

Let us pray that we shall be able to welcome Jesus at Christmas, not in the cold manger of a selfish heart, but in a heart full of love, compassion, joy and peace, a heart warm with love for one another.
  —Mother Teresa

19

†

His Law is Love and His Gospel is Peace

Love and peace. They seem to go together, don't they? If we don't love, we can't possibly have peace. And if we don't have peace, we find it difficult to love. Yet, if we have one of those attributes—just one—it automatically leads us to practice the other also. It's inevitable.

Like peanut butter and jelly, husband and wife, cookies and milk, Tom and Jerry, hugs and kisses, and all sorts of combinations, love and peace go hand-in-hand. If you stop loving, you won't have peace. And, if you shun peace, you're unable to love. It's as simple as that.

On that first Christmas, God demonstrated both love and peace. First of all, the Bible tells us, "God is love" (1 John 4:8 and 16). God is not only the originator of love and the essence of love. He's the promoter of it. "We love because He first loved us" (1 John 4:19). He loved us so much He sent His only begotten Son to perform the most extraordinary form of reconciliation between God and man.

Because we have experienced God's unconditional love, we are equipped to extend unconditional love to others. We receive His love vertically, and we transfer it horizontally. Romans 5:5 says, "The love of God is shed abroad in our hearts by the Holy Ghost which is given to us." See? God has already given us the means to extend love, even to the unlovable. He gifted us with His Holy Spirit, the administrator of all good things.

God also called us to peace. The scriptures talk about "the peace which passeth all understanding" (Philippians 4:7) and "perfect peace ... because he trusteth in Thee" (Isaiah 26:3). God wants us to love others and to live in peace with others. Romans Chapter 12 is full of verses that tell us how to practice love and peace.

The chapter begins with us being transformed (verse 2). From that starting point we become humble (verses 3, 10, and 16), hospitable (verse 13), compassionate (verse 15) and giving (verse 20). If we practice the gifts God has bestowed on us, the result has to reveal both love and peace.

God was our perfect example. He exercised both love and peace on the night Jesus was born. The angels declared, "Glory to God in the highest, and on earth peace, good will toward men" (Luke 2:14).

God demonstrated His love toward us by giving His Son as a sacrifice for our sins. The scriptures remind us of this truth. "But God commendeth his love toward us, in that, while we were yet sinners, Christ died for us" (Romans 5:8).

God did something most people—especially those of us who are parents—would find appalling. He gave His firstborn Son to be sacrificed on behalf of worthless sinners. That's an unfathomable expression of love. God loved us so much, He did the unbelievable.

At the same time, God demonstrated His desire to make peace with His fallen creation. Consider how many centuries passed before Jesus came to resolve the enmity between man and his Creator. God practiced incredible patience as, century after century, man did what he thought was right in his own eyes and ignored God's laws completely. People still do that. Then, when things go bad, who do they turn to? You guessed it, the only One who can bail them out of their troubles. Their Father in heaven. The One who sacrificed His only Son, Jesus, so that one day, the wayward souls would turn to Him.

We see it happening every time there's a catastrophe. There's a school shooting, and the next day the front page of the newspaper has a photo of teenagers gathered in prayer around the flagpole. Enemy planes attack the twin towers in New York City. The next Sunday, the churches are full of prayer warriors. Even in our own homes, when we're caught up in everyday responsibilities, we sometimes get a bit lax about prayer times. Then, tragedy strikes and we're on our knees.

But God knows the human heart. He understands our frailties and He forgives. He doesn't depart from us. We depart from Him. He is faithful. He's still here, offering love and peace. You only have to reach out and receive his free gift. And then extend it to others.

Moment of Reflection: Are you at peace? Not only with others, but with yourself? Does the Word of God bless you with feelings of peace and love? If so, then you've been commissioned to offer God's love and peace to others. God has placed you in a mission field. It could be your home or your school or your workplace. It could be your neighborhood. Is there someone you need to love more? Do you need to make peace with someone? Don't let another day go by before you do so.

Every place you live will be a Bethlehem, and every day you live will be a Christmas. You, like Mary, will deliver Christ into the world.
—Max Lucado, Grace for the Moment

20

†

CHAINS SHALL HE BREAK, FOR THE SLAVE IS OUR BROTHER

This line brings to mind two men who fought against slavery in the late 18th century. One was William Wilberforce, a British politician and Christian who, for nearly two decades, spoke up against slavery during sessions of Parliament.

The other was an Englishman who at one time in his life was captain of a slave ship. His name was John Newton. During a terrible storm that threatened to sink his ship, Newton was converted to Christianity. As he cried out to God for mercy, he also was convicted about his role in the slave trade business.

Moved to tears, Newton wrote the poem that became the popular hymn "Amazing Grace." He quit the slave trade and gave his support to William Wilberforce in his attempt to end slavery altogether.

Just as chains were broken the day the House of Commons passed the bill to end slavery in Britain, so also did the chains of spiritual bondage drop from John Newton's heart.

But Newton wasn't all that different from so many people who are bound by the chains of materialism and self-serving lifestyles. We see them every day. On city streets. In the classrooms and workplaces. Sometimes in our own families.

They walk around doing their own thing, sometimes in sin,

sometimes not sinning but totally oblivious of how their materialism and self-centeredness are keeping them chained.

Do you know someone who is bound by such chains? Are you one of them? Whether it's you or someone dear, you have the power to remove those chains. Jesus came to earth holding the keys of freedom in his hand.

When we look at a manger scene, we hardly believe a helpless little baby would have the power to release us from bondage. But that's the whole reason Jesus took on human form. As a human He subjected Himself to the same temptations and materialistic lures we face. The difference is He resisted them. Try as we might, we cannot do the same under our own power. We need His help and the guidance of the Holy Spirit.

Jesus didn't leave us stranded. He offered the keys to our release. He said, "And ye shall know the truth, and the truth shall make you free" (John 8:32). That's key number one. Truth. The lies of the devil will keep us chained. The truth Christ offers will break those chains and set us free. And how do we acquire that truth? Before His crucifixion, Jesus said, "I am the way, the truth, and the life: no man cometh unto the Father, but by me" (John 14:6). That's how we break the chains.

Key number two involves knowing God's word and following it. Jesus said, "If ye love me, keep my commandments" (John 14:14). Sounds easy, doesn't it? The truth is, we struggle daily to obey God's word. The rebellious spirit inside us keeps dragging us back to our self-imposed prison cell. It's always been that way with mankind since the time of Adam and Eve.

But God devised a way to unlock those chains of spiritual bondage. It happened the day Jesus went to the cross. From that moment, the chains began to slip away. One-by-one Jesus unlocks the chains and sets people free. So if you know someone who's living in bondage, or if you yourself are bound by chains of any kind—whether it be sin or despair or frustration or disappointment or lack of confidence—you can break the chains. Jesus has the keys and He's holding them out to you.

Moment of Reflection: Are you closed off by the chains of sin and selfish living? Or are the chains of defeat and despair holding you captive? Turn to the manger and consider the child God sent to remove those chains. Next, turn to the cross and see how He did it. If you haven't already put your trust in the Savior, do it now. Offer Him your chains. He'll break them away. His truth will set you free.

God's time is always near. He set the North Star in the heavens; He gave me the strength in my limbs; He meant I should be free.
–*Harriet Tubman*

21

†

And in His Name All Oppression Shall Cease

Everybody has a name. Sometimes, we're named after parents or grandparents or some other favorite relative. Our names are personal. They set us apart from everyone else. They're our identity. Our labels. And, unless we change them legally, they stay with us for our entire lives. Good or bad, we're stuck with them.

Some names are memorable. Like George Washington and Bill Gates and Mick Jagger. They don't need any explanation. Each name conjures up a different image. Some remind us of people we associated with long ago, or they invoke a memory of a life-changing event. Sometimes those memories are precious, sometimes they're painful. The sound of a name brings a different memory or emotion. For example, if I hear the name Walt Disney, I think of animated films and theme parks and a man who's been frozen somewhere. His name makes me smile.

If I hear the name Ronald McDonald, I think of golden arches and French fries and a house where parents can be near their sick child who is going through treatments.

But what about names like Adolph Hitler and Charles Manson and Judas Iscariot? Don't those names leave a bitter taste in your mouth? The image behind those names is one of oppression and murder and evil personified.

In contrast, there's a name that carries with it a sense of goodness and love and comfort. A name that soothes the heart, clears the mind, and offers peace and good will. It's a powerful name. You guessed it. It's Jesus.

Nothing troubles me more than to hear my Lord's name spoken in jest or as a curse word. His name is precious. We need to speak it with reverence. The same goes for the name of God. One of the Ten Commandments says, "Thou shalt not take the name of the Lord thy God in vain" (Exodus 20:7). I'm offended when movie actors think it's okay to use God's name in a negative way, even in PG movies when it's least expected. It's not because I'm so perfect. I'm far from perfect. It's because I have respect for the name of my Lord. As I said, His name is precious.

My daughter Vicki likes to listen to Hillsong Worship's version of "What a Beautiful Name it is, the name of Jesus Christ the King." She has a CD player and a karaoke machine in her bedroom. Sometimes, I hear her singing through her closed bedroom door. Vicki has Down syndrome. She also has a childlike love of Jesus and a faith I believe could move mountains. Yet, Vicki doesn't seek a miracle. She's content to simply sing praises to her God and Savior.

Vicki accepted Christ as her "best friend" during Vacation Bible School. She was baptized at Church @ the Springs in Ocala. When the baptizer asked her if she had made Jesus her special friend, she proudly shouted, "Yes, I have." There wasn't a dry eye in the building.

Vicki smiles when she says the name of Jesus. In her innocence she connects with God in a way that eludes many of us. Jesus said we should come to Him like little children. Vicki's already doing that. We do too whenever we approach Him in an attitude of humility and trust.

Yes, there is beauty and wonder and power in the name of Jesus. We say a blessing over a meal and we end with the words, "In Jesus' name." We pray in His name when a loved one is ill, when a job is at stake, when a relationship is in trouble. We thank Him for unexpected blessings. And, we can seek miracles and help in time of trouble for ourselves and for others, always in His name and, hopefully, according to the Father's will.

The scriptures speak of the wonder-working power of Jesus' name. In salvation: "For whosoever shall call upon the name of the Lord shall be saved" (Romans 10:13). In our daily lives: "And whatsoever ye do in word or deed, do all in the name of the Lord Jesus" (Colossians 3:17). In gratitude: "Giving thanks always for all things unto God and the Father in the name of our Lord Jesus Christ" (Ephesians 5:20).

The Son of God was given many names throughout the Bible, but at the time of His birth, two names had profound meanings that stand out at Christmas time and all year through. Immanuel, as prophesied in Isaiah 7:14, meaning "God With Us," and the name given at the time of the Lord's circumcision in Luke 2:21, was Jesus, meaning "Savior." As you go about your holiday routines, remember those two names, and hold them in high regard, for He is with us and He came to save us.

Moment of Reflection: A word of caution. Don't call on Jesus' name as a mantra or an incantation to get whatever you want. Jesus prayed with the Father's will in mind, and so should we. Treasure Jesus' name, connect with Him, and build a relationship with Him. There isn't a better way to fall asleep at night than with the name of Jesus on your lips.

How deeply we who love the Lord of Love and desire to follow him long for the power to surmount all difficulties and tests and conflicts in life in the same exultant and triumphant way.
–Hannah Hurnard, Hinds' Feet in High Places

22

†

Sweet Hymns of Joy in Grateful Chorus Raise We

"O Holy Night" isn't the only popular Christmas song. Our hymn books are full of wonderful carols. Several favorites come immediately to mind. "O Come, All Ye Faithful," "Silent Night," "Away in a Manger," "Joy to the World," and multiple other yuletide offerings that focus on the birth of Jesus Christ.

"Silent Night" mentions the night of our dear Savior's birth. I don't know if the night was silent or not, but the song says it was silent. The shepherds were probably so awestruck they couldn't speak. Other than the baaing of their sheep and then the angels' voices, it could have been a very silent night. If Joseph Mohr, the writer of "Silent Night," wanted to say it was silent way back in 1816, that's okay with me. It kind of sets a mood, doesn't it. I imagine at least one moment of silence happened when the shepherds first saw the Christ child. The sight of the newborn king must have taken their breath away.

The song also gives us a few details about the birth of Christ. "'Round yon virgin, mother and child" puts the focus on the mother-child relationship. Can you imagine how Mary felt, after nine long months, to actually hold the Son of God in her arms? She knew in advance what her role would be. The angel had told her, and she had agreed to be used by God for this purpose.

What about "Away in a Manger" as a Christmas song? Mangers were dirty bins or holes carved out of a rock wall. The stable might not have been a wooden structure at all, but perhaps a cave, though our nativity scenes depict it more like a modern-day barn. Bethlehem was built on a limestone hillside. The inn would probably have been upstairs and a cave underneath would have housed the innkeeper's animals, maybe a donkey and a couple of goats. More likely, the animals would have been grazing in a field. Many Bible scholars believe it wasn't winter at all but probably late spring or early summer.

Such was the environment that welcomed Jesus into the world. The innkeeper said he had no room. The town was overrun with people who had come from many places in obedience to the Roman census. Do you suppose if the innkeeper knew he was turning away the Messiah he might have made room for the holy family? He even would have given up his own bed.

What about you? Do you have room in your daily routine for the Savior of the world? Do you relegate Him to a dimly lit corner of your heart, the same way you set up your nativity scene? Do you visit Him often through His Word, spend time with Him before you start your day? I once heard a Christian school teacher named Sharon Loyd say that if she didn't spend time with God before heading out to her job every morning she would be cheating everyone who came in contact with her for the rest of the day.

What a great example we all should follow, not only at Christmas time, but always. At least 15 minutes or more in the Word every morning can affect the rest of our day. It can fortify us for whatever comes, prepare us for conversations with others, and instill in us a sense of peace, no matter what trouble may come.

So, at Christmas, we have some wonderful hymns to keep us in a godly mood. "O Holy Night" and "Silent Night" create a quiet, meditative atmosphere. "Away in a Manger" focuses on the baby.

Like the shepherds and the wise men, we are drawn to the holy place of Christ's birth.

When we want to express gratitude for the gift of salvation the Christ child offers, we belt out the lyrics to "O Come All Ye Faithful," and "Joy to the World." Those songs invite us to the manger in a celebratory expression of faith.

What do you think about when you sing those Christmas carols? Have you memorized them so well they've become vain repetitions? Pay attention to the words. They offer a wonderful escape from the hectic activities surrounding the holiday. While the materialistic world around us hawks the next big sale and songs like "Jingle Bells" and "Santa Claus is Coming to Town" say nothing about the birth of the Savior, the inspirational carols bring us back to the true meaning of Christmas. Isn't it time, as some say, to put "Christ" back in Christmas?

Moment of Reflection: Consider dropping all the fuss and just get together with friends for a night of Christmas caroling in your neighborhood or downtown at the public square. Or, gather in someone's home for hot chocolate and an hour of singing carols. Why not choose a Christmas hymn to sing right now, all by yourself. Perhaps it will be a holy night after all.

I think every songwriter has written a Christmas song. But no one will ever write a better one than "O Holy Night," about the birth of Christ. It is perfection!
—*Bobby Goldsboro, Entertainer/Fine Artist*

23

†

Let All Within Us Praise His Holy Name!

The shepherds left their flocks and hurried to Bethlehem. As soon as they arrived, the manger was no longer a crib for a newborn child. It had become a place of worship. It was an altar. And on it was the Lamb of God.

We don't know how many shepherds showed up. It could have been a handful or it could have been a huge gathering. It doesn't matter how many were there. The point is, worship can take place with only one person or a roomful, or it could involve a large cathedral full of worshipers. Sometimes, worship begins with only one person speaking or singing praises. Then others catch on, and still more join in, until multitudes raise their voices.

A wonderful example of such a progression can be seen in the Book of Revelation.

In the first chapter, John experiences a vision of Jesus in glowing attire with a two-edged sword coming out of His mouth. What does John immediately do? Look at Revelation 1:17: "And when I saw him, I fell at his feet as dead." Now that's worship! One man fell to the floor in complete submission before a vision "of the Alpha and Omega, the First and the Last, the One who was alive and died and lives forevermore" (verse 18).

You don't need to be sitting in a huge cathedral to worship Jesus.

You can do so in the privacy of your own bedroom, or when taking a shower, or while driving your car. One person worshiping has just as much of a connection with God as an entire church does.

But, the worship by one can certainly grow and spread.

Take a look at Revelation Chapter 4. Again, it's John, now standing before a vision of the throne with four beasts in the midst. And what are those beasts doing? They're worshiping, saying, "Holy, holy, holy, Lord God Almighty, which was, and is, and is to come" (Revelation 4:8). Now the number of worshipers has grown from one to four—or five, if you want to count John. I can't imagine him just standing there while the four beasts are worshiping the Lord, can you?

This situation may be an example of what happens when two or more are gathered in the name of Jesus. Didn't He promise He would be there in their midst?

Further on in Revelation 4:10-11, the twenty-four elders fall down and worship, saying, "Thou art worthy, O Lord, to receive glory and honour and power: for thou hast created all things, and for thy pleasure they are and were created."

See how the number has grown? Now, it's not just John and it's not just the four beasts. Now twenty-four people are worshiping the Lord and casting their crowns before His throne. This is like a home team of people who gather during the week for fellowship, prayer, and to study the word of God. They also are worshiping.

In Revelation Chapter 5 the number grows even more, when many angels join the four beasts and the twenty-four elders in worship. What do verses 11-12 say the number was? "Ten thousand times ten thousand, and thousands of thousands, Saying with a loud voice, Worthy is the Lamb that was slain to receive power, and riches, and wisdom, and strength, and honour, and glory, and blessing."

That's not just one church, unless it's a really big mega-church, but it may be thousands of churches. Can you imagine what it's like in heaven on Sunday morning when millions of congregations around the world send up their voices in song, many of them at the same time? Our omniscient God hears them all.

But the number can grow even more than that. Look at Revelation 7:9-12, which speaks of "a great multitude, which no man could number, of all nations, and kindreds, and people, and tongues." This is like a worldwide revival! They are clothed in white robes and they are singing praises in a LOUD voice, "Salvation to our God which sitteth upon the throne, and unto the Lamb." Then the angels join in and proclaim, "Amen: Blessing, and glory, and wisdom, and thanksgiving, and honour, and power, and might, be unto our God for ever and ever. Amen."

So, we've gone from one person falling on his face to an unfathomable number of worshipers. Wouldn't you like to join their song, today and again someday in heaven?

Moment of Reflection: Worship can involve only one person or it can involve many. It can take place in someone's home or in a church or in a huge auditorium, or even on a city street. The focus shouldn't be on the worshipers. It's in honor of Jesus Christ. Consider this: wherever you are when you're singing hymns of worship, you just may be joining a host of unseen white-robed angels who are worshiping at that very same moment before the Lamb's throne.

What is the glory of God? It is who God is. It is the essence of His nature; the weight of His importance; the radiance of His splendor; the demonstration of His power; the atmosphere of His presence.
—Rick Warren, pastor of Saddleback Church
author of The Purpose Driven Life

24

✝

CHRIST IS THE LORD, THEN EVER! EVER PRAISE WE!

Forever is a long, long time, isn't it? Forever encompasses not only the future but also the past and the present. It's mind-boggling to imagine Jesus having existed before time began. He is the Alpha and Omega, the first and the last. He's eternal, living forever, with no beginning and no end. And He will continue to exist long after this world is gone.

The Lord wants us to join Him in His eternal kingdom. He's laid eternity out in front of us. He's qualified to make this amazing offer. He paid for it on the cross of Calvary. All we need to do is accept Him and what He has accomplished through His death and resurrection. We don't have to work for eternal life. We can't earn it. We can't buy it. Salvation is a free gift. A Christmas gift.

Time doesn't matter to God. He doesn't have a grandfather clock in His house of many mansions. He doesn't wear a wristwatch. He doesn't use a timer or a stopwatch or an alarm clock. He always was and always will be, so time has no place in His kingdom.

Jesus had a brief thirty-three years on earth as a human being, but that's a mere drop in the pool of eternity. Doesn't the Bible say, "Jesus Christ the same yesterday, and today, and forever" in Hebrews 13:8? So the babe in the manger had a limited time to live as a human being, but as God He is eternal, and through His death on the cross He offers us the same thing.

Sometimes, it's hard for us to think beyond this present realm. Here on earth we worry about time every day of our lives. Will we be late for work? Will we be on time for church? Will we get to school before the bell rings? Will we be ready for a date? How about that party Saturday night? Or the football game? We want to get a good seat.

Then there are deadlines. We work all week with deadlines breathing down our necks. The pressure builds up. We burn the candle at both ends. Time is controlling our lives.

And birthdays and anniversaries? Which number are we celebrating this year? How many more numbers do we have left? Only God knows.

Look beyond this brief life—James called it "a vapor, that appeareth for a little time" (there's that word "time" again), "and then vanisheth away" (James 4:14). Open your heart to that wondrous taste of forever God has promised to those who believe in His Son.

The scriptures also seem concerned with beginnings. Two books in the Bible start with the words "In the beginning." One is Genesis 1:1 where it says "In the beginning God created the heaven and the earth." The chapter goes on to describe all of the things God created.

The other mention of "the beginning" is in the Gospel of John. Chapter One starts this way: "In the beginning was the Word, and the Word was with God, and the Word was God."

So, the Word was with God in the beginning and took part in the creation of the world. And who was that Word? John 1:14 says, "The Word was made flesh, and dwelt among us."

Sounds like Jesus, doesn't it? Colossians 1:16 affirms that all things were created by Him. The babe in the manger had been around for a long, long time. He was involved in creation along with God and the Holy Spirit (Genesis 1:2). Everything was made by the Father, the Son, and the Holy Spirit. The materials for the book in your hands, the chair you're sitting on, and the lamp that is casting light on the page you're reading all came from natural products created by the Holy Trinity.

If that doesn't put you in an attitude of praise and thankfulness this Christmas, I don't know what will. Christ is the Lord! Praise His holy name forever. Praise Him in the morning. Praise Him in the evening. He is God in the flesh. He is the Creator of all things.

It's not just about loving the child in the manger. It's about loving the Savior who sacrificed His life on your behalf. It's about the One who miraculously rose from the dead, the Resurrected One who ascended into heaven, the King who sits on the throne. All of those images make up one person, and that one person isn't bound by time. It's irrelevant, immaterial, unnecessary in the place where He has gone. And one day His followers will shed their watches and clocks and they'll discard their schedules and Post-it notes, and they'll bask in the glory of a timeless eternity.

Moment of Reflection: It's time to stop thinking about time. Look beyond the years you may have left on this earth and focus your attention on the place that has no temporal limitations. Imagine living forever. And, don't worry. It won't be boring. You'll have plenty to do and plenty to be thankful for in that great and timeless expanse called heaven.

Glory in Christ and you can bask in His light forever.
—Woodrow Kroll

25

†

His Pow'r and Glory, Evermore Proclaim!
His Pow'r and Glory, Evermore Proclaim!

Power and glory. Two attributes among many that belong to God.

Did the baby in the manger know He already possessed these qualities? That He had power from above? That glory would ultimately be His?

Surely, those shepherds and wise men must have known something was gloriously different about that child. Otherwise, why did they leave their responsibilities and go to Bethlehem? Why did the shepherds believe the angels who spoke to them? Why didn't they brush off the heavenly visit as a hallucination? Why did they leave their flock to go see a baby in a manger? Didn't that sound ridiculous? Most people would think so.

At that time in history, Rome had taken over the land. The Jews lived under the stringent rules of Caesar. They were being taxed. They had restrictions. The Romans oppressed many of the Jews, even made some of them slaves.

But the Jews also knew the prophecies. They had grown up hearing about the promise of a Messiah. Isaiah spoke about a virgin birth and the coming of Emmanuel which means "God With Us" (Matthew 1:23). The prophet Micah said the promised one would come out of Bethlehem (Micah 5:2). The entire Jewish world was waiting for their Messiah to come and rescue them. A heavenly array of angels told the shepherds that the great, longed-for event had finally happened. Of course, they went "with haste" to see this babe, as it says in Luke 2:16.

And, after they'd visited the place where Jesus was born, didn't they run off and proclaim the wonderful event to all who would listen? Apparently, they were the first missionaries to go out and tell the good news.

And, what about the wise men? Why would anyone travel with a load of precious gifts over dusty roads in areas where bandits lurked in the hills, and food and water were scarce? Why did they leave their homes, their wives, their children, and their work, in order to follow a bright light in the sky? They must have had some foreknowledge that something great was about to happen. These were supposed to be *wise* men. They weren't naive idiots who could be drawn great distances by the fortune tellers and scam artists of their day. They had a purpose.

These men may have been Gentiles, yet somehow they knew about the Jewish prophecy. And after meeting with King Herod, they received a warning in a dream telling them not to return to the palace with a report where to find the child. They left by a different route. By the time Herod figured things out, the wise men had departed and so had the Holy Family (Matthew 2:12-15).

So, we have poor shepherds and wealthy wise men—two extremes in the economical sphere of that day. People from those two extremes had the privilege of being among the first to witness one of the greatest events in history—the birth of Jesus Christ, Son of God and Savior.

Even today, God reaches out to a mix of social classes. Rich and poor, weak and strong, leaders and followers, everyone has the chance to know the Savior. Every city in America has at least one church. I can think of a couple of Florida towns that have a main intersection with a church on every corner. As some residents jokingly say, "You can throw a stone in any direction and break a stained-glass window." A church on every corner. And, in some cities, multiple churches on multiple corners. There is no excuse for Americans never to have heard the message of salvation. Even if they don't attend a church, they can hear God's word on TV and the radio. It's sometimes quoted in newspapers and magazines. It's all around us.

American missionaries run off to other countries, and that's a good thing too. Those people are hungry for the word of God. In Papua New Guinea, tribesmen have been known to travel for three days out of dense jungle and beg for missionaries to come to their villages and tell their people about the promise of God's Son.

Yet, here in America, people take that vital message for granted, or they simply ignore it. They're too busy, too caught up in their work and making money and more money and more money. But there is another kind of wealth money can't buy. It's a pearl of great price, a spiritual treasure, and it promises eternal life. From the manger to the cross, the message is always the same. Someone in your realm needs to hear it.

Moment of Reflection: As you go about your daily chores and get your home ready for the holidays, turn aside now and then from the tinsel and the lights and from the nativity scene. Find a quiet place to reflect on the One who is at the heart of the Christmas season. Then, take the message to others within your sphere of influence and beyond. That is the best way to praise God, by telling someone else what He has done.

King of Kings and Lord of Lords And He shall reign forever and ever.
George Frideric Handel, Hallelujah Chorus, Messiah

Conclusion

My prayer is that the lyrics to "O Holy Night" and this devotional gift book will bless your heart during this Christmas season. My goal was to keep the focus where it should be, on the birth of Jesus Christ. The world would have us change the name from "Christmas" to "the holidays" or some other generic term that threatens to diminish the true meaning of the season.

Every day, from October on, we are inundated with the material side of the season, and while that's not altogether bad, it does tend to distract us from the real meaning of Christmas.

It's true, we don't know the exact date when Jesus was born. Churches over the years have been celebrating the event in December, but it could very well have taken place in the summer. The main thing is that we remember, year after year, that there was a moment in time when our Lord and Savior left His throne in heaven and came to earth to rescue us from our sins and from our pain.

Now that is something to celebrate.

May this Christmas bring joy and peace to your life and to the lives of your loved ones.

Merry Christmas!

Acknowledgements

First, I thank my Lord and Savior Jesus Christ for coming to earth as a human baby and offering His mercy and grace and the gift of eternal life. May this book bring glory to His name!

I also thank my dear friend and sister in Christ, Delores Kight, for her editing skills.

Thanks to my proof readers, my daughter Joanna Jones and my granddaughter Zelda Jones.

I also recognize Joanna for using her artistic skills to create a simple yet elegant cover.

Finally, my appreciation to Mike Parker and WordCrafts Press for bringing this book to publication.

The following references provided information and/or permissions of use:

The Lyrics: https://www.classicfm.com/discover-music/occasions/christmas/o-holy-night-original-lyrics-composer-recordings/

Introduction: beliefnet.com/entertainment/movies/the-nativity-story/the-amazing-story-of-o-holy-night.aspx. also https://www.godtube.com/popular-hymns/o-holy-night-lyrics-story-behind-carol/ and https://www.irelandsown.ie/the-story-behind-o-holy-night-2/

Chapter 1: Mario Villella quote: goodnewsocala.com/sermons/o-holy-night/4-it-is-the-night-of-our-dear-saviors-birth.

Chapter 2: Kirk Cameron quote: Permission by Kirk Cameron, re: Zach Legat, CamFam Studios.

Chapter 3: Bob Hostetler/Josh McDowell quote: taken from The One Year Book of Josh McDowell's Family Devotions by Bob Hostetler and Josh D. McDowell. Copyright © 1997. Used by permission of Tyndale House Publishers, a Division of Tyndale House Ministries. All rights reserved.

Chapter 4: https://www.godtube.com/popular-hymns/amazing-grace/;

Charles H. Spurgeon quote: Taken from Morning & Evening by Charles H. Spurgeon, Copyright © 1980 by Charles H. Spurgeon. Used by permission of Zondervan. www.zondervan.com.

Chapter 5: Charles Stanley quote: Taken from God's Way, Day By Day by Charles F. Stanley, Copyright ©, 2004. Used by permission of Thomas Nelson.

Chapter 6: Steve Saint quote: https://www.azquotes.com/quote/721971; Used by permission of Steve Saint.

Chapter 7: https://www.umcdiscipleship.org/resources/history-of-hymns-morning-has-broken; https://www.songfacts.com/facts/cat-stevens/morning-has-broken;

Linda Hang quote: Taken from Unfinished, Devotions & Prayers for a Heart Under Construction; Copyright © 2018. Used by permission of Barbour Publishing Inc.

Chapter 8: https://www.countrythangdaily.com/remind-dear-lord-hymn-will-remind-goodness-highest-almighty/

Joseph Carroll quote: Taken from How To Worship Jesus Christ, Copyright © 2013. Used by permission of Moody Publishers.

Chapter 9: Billy Graham quote: https://www.brainyquote.com/quotes/billy_graham_384204; Included with permission by The Billy Graham Literary Trust, per: Christian P. Cherry PLLC, Charlotte, N.C.

Chapter 10: Norman Vincent Peale quote: Used by permission from the Peale Foundation, Pawling Office, Brian L. Berlandi, Esq.; also noted on

ACKNOWLEDGEMENTS

allchristianquotes.org/authors/162/Norman_Vincent_Peale.

Chapter 11: Og Mandino quote: Used by permission of The Og Mandino Leadership Institute, per: Dave Blanchard; also noted on https://www.brainyquote.com/quotes/og_mandino_140597.

Chapter 12: Mrs. Charles E. Cowman quote: Taken from Streams in the Desert by Mrs. Charles E. Cowman, Copyright © 1965. Used by permission of Daybreak Books, Zondervan. www.zondervan.com.

Chapter 13: https://www.jewishvirtuallibrary.org/perea-gilead; Expository Dictionary of New Testament Words, W.E. Vine, published by Revell Co. and The Analytical Greek Lexicon Revised 1978 edition, ed. by Harold K. Mouton, Published by Zondervan Publishing House;

Henry Wadsworth Longfellow quote: Taken from The Three Kings, https://www.public-domain-poetry.com/henry-wadsworth-longfellow/three-kings-24346.

Chapter 14: Harper's Bible Dictionary, Madeleine S. Miller and J. Lane Miller, Harper & Row, Publishers, New York, 1973;

Oswald Chambers quote: Taken from My Utmost for His Highest® by Oswald Chambers, © l935 by Dodd Mead & Co., renewed © 1963 by the Oswald Chambers Publications Assn., Ltd., and is used by permission of Discovery House Publishers, Box 3566, Grand Rapids MI 4950l. All rights reserved.

Chapter 15: www.stempublishing.com/hymns/biographies/scriven.html and https://reasonabletheology.org/hymn-story-friend-jesus/

What a Friend We Have in Jesus: https://www.hopepublishing.com/find-hymns-hw/hw5607.aspx

Madame Guyon quote: Taken from a poem titled God's Glory and Goodness in Union With God/22 of Madame Guyon's Poems. Copyright © 1975. Used by permission from Seed Sowers Christian Books, Jacksonville. books@seedsowers.com.

Chapter 16: George Whitefield quote: Taken from "What Think Ye of Christ"

from The Sermons of George Whitefield, © 2012 by the Church Society, pp. 87. Used by permission of Crossway, a publishing ministry of Good News Publishers, Wheaton, IL, 60187. www.crossway.org.

Chapter 17: https://www.thegospelcoalition.org/blogs/justin-taylor/charles-wesleys-and-can-it-be-background-and-scriptural-allusions/ and http://www.fivecrowns.com/five-crowns-of-salvation-2/

A.W. Tozer quote: Taken from The Pursuit of God, Copyright © 1948. Used by permission of Aneko Press/Life Sentencing Publication.

Chapter 18: Mother Teresa quote: The writings of Mother Teresa of Calcutta copyright © by the Mother Teresa Center, exclusive licensee throughout the world of the Missionaries of Charity for the words of Mother Teresa, Used with permission.

Chapter 19: Max Lucado quote: Taken from Grace for the Moment, Volume II, by Max Lucado, Copyright © 2006. Used by permission of Thomas Nelson. www.thomasnelson.com.

Chapter 20: www.bbc.co.uk/history/historic figures/wilberforce william.shtml; https://banneroftruth.org/us/resources/articles/2001/john-newtons-conversion/

https://genius.com/John-newton-amazing-grace-annotated.

Harriet Tubman quote: Harriet Tubman to Ednah Dow Cheney, New York City, circa 1859, cited with approval of the Harriet Tubman Historical Society, June 25, 2020, http://www.harriet-tubman.org. Much of the information from this site is based on "Harriet Tubman, The Road to Freedom" by Catherine Clinton, "Scenes in the Life of Harriet Tubman" by Sarah Hopkins Bradford, and "Bound for the Promised Land: Harriet Tubman: Portrait of an American Hero" by Kate Clifford Larson.

Chapter 21: Jesus' name, "Savior," from https://www.christianity.com/jesus/is-jesus-god/names-of-jesus/what-does-the-name-jesus-mean.html

Hannah Hurnard quote: Taken from Hinds' Feet on High Places by Hannah

ACKNOWLEDGEMENTS

Hurnard. Copyright © 1986. Used by permission of Tyndale House Publishers, a Division of Tyndale House Ministries. All rights reserved.

Chapter 22: https://www.wrti.org/post/story-behind-beloved-christmas-carol-silent-night;

Bobby Goldsboro quote: Used by permission of Bobby Goldsboro, Entertainer/Fine Artist

Chapter 23: Rick Warren quote: Taken from Purpose Driven Life, Day 7, Copyright © 2002. Zondervan Publishing, Grand Rapids. Used by permission also from the office of Pastor Rick Warren, Saddleback Church. www.saddleback.com.

Chapter 24: Woodrow Kroll quote: Used by permission from Woodrow Kroll, Creator of The HELIOS Projects; Radio host, Back to the Bible

Chapter 25: https://genius.com/George-frideric-handel-the-messiah-hallelujah-lyrics

About the Author

Marian Rizzo has won numerous awards in the field of journalism, including the New York Times Chairman's Award and first place in the 2015 Amy Foundation Writing Awards. She also was nominated for a Pulitzer Prize in the category of explanatory journalism.

Marian worked for the Ocala Star-Banner newspaper for 30 years. She also has written several magazine articles for "Ocala Style Magazine" and Billy Graham's "Decision Magazine."

Several of Marian's novels have won first-place awards at conferences and retreats. Three of her books were named on Amazon's Best Seller and Hot New Releases charts. Her suspense novel, *Muldovah,* was a finalist in the 2018 Genesis competition at the American Christian Writers Association Conference.

Marian earned a bachelor's degree in Bible education from Luther Rice Seminary. She trained for jungle missions with New Tribes Mission (now ETHNOS 360), and served for two semesters at a Youth With A Mission training center in southern Spain.

Marian lives in Ocala, Florida, with her daughter, Vicki, who has Down syndrome. Her other daughter, Joanna, has blessed her with three wonderful grandchildren.

Visit Marian online at MariansCorner.com.

✝

Also Available From
Marian Rizzo

Angela's Treasures
In Search of the Beloved
Muldovah
In Search of Felicity
Presence in the Pew
The Leper

Also Available From
WordCrafts Press

Grace Extended by Paula K. Parker
Morning Mist by Barbie Loflin
A Revelation of Love by Jill Grossman
The Power of Hope by Patty Mason

www.WordCrafts.net

www.ingramcontent.com/pod-product-compliance
Lightning Source LLC
Chambersburg PA
CBHW072040110526
44592CB00012B/1496